LADLED

NOURISHING SOUPS FOR ALL SEASONS

Kimberly Harris

VICTORY BELT PUBLISHING INC.
Las Vegas

First Published in 2012 by Victory Belt Publishing Inc.

ISBN 13: 978-1-936608-67-6

Printed in The USA
RRD1210

Dedication

*To my little family,
thank you for making
my life beautiful
and sweet.*

*Special thanks to Elena
for eating soup alongside her momma
these last 5 years.*

Table of Contents

Thumbnail Recipe
Table of Contents

6

Fresh Corn Soup
152

Roasted Garlic and Potato Soup
154

(Dark) Green Soup
156

SOUPS
CENTERED
ON LEGUMES
AND GRAINS

Egyptian Red Lentil Soup with Caramelized Onions
160

Mexican Black Bean Soup
162

Fava Bean and Vegetable Soup with Pesto
164

Easy Chicken and Rice Soup
166

Buckwheat and Root Vegetable Soup with Meatballs
168

Simple Lentil Soup
170

Simple Split Pea Soup
172

Cock-a-Leekie
174

Garlicky White Bean Soup with Dark Greens
176

French Lentil and Vegetable Soup with Pesto
178

Quinoa and Chicken Soup
180

Moroccan Fava and Vegetable Soup
182

Smokey Lentil and Chicken Soup with Dark Greens
184

HEARTY
SOUPS
AND
STEWS

Curried Beef Stew
188

Chicken and Shrimp Gumbo
190

Caramelized Onion and Potato Soup
192

Roasted Tomato and Bread Soup
194

Garam Masala Chickpea Stew
196

Oxtail Stew with Red Wine
198

Scotch Broth
200

Turkey and Wild Rice Soup
202

British Beef Stew with Dumplings
204

Spring Chicken Soup
206

Leek and Potato Soup
208

Pot-au-Feu
210

212
Chicken and
Dumplings

214
Italian Vegetable and
Sausage Soup

216
Lamb Stew

218
Jamaican Oxtail Soup

SEAFOOD
SOUPS

224
Lemongrass Clam
Chowder

226
Simple White Fish and
Rice Soup

228
Mussels in Tomato
Garlic Broth

230
White Fish Soup with
Fennel, Green Beans, and
Tomatoes

232
Poor Man's
Bouillabaisse

234
Creamy Salmon
Chowder

236
Clams in a Spicy Tomato
Broth with Bacon

GRAIN
PORRIDGES
AND RICE
CONGEES

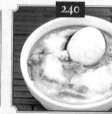
240
Chinese Congee
(Zhou)

242
Thai Rice Congee
(Chok)

244
Japanese Congee with
Soy Ginger Salmon

246
Miso Brown Rice
Congee

248
Simple Brown Rice
Congee and Variations

250
Korean Sesame Seed
Porridge

252
Irish Yellow Broth

254
Spiced Moroccan Millet
Porridge with Milk

CHILLED
SOUPS

258
Tangy Basil Lettuce
Soup

260
Chilled Avocado and
Cucumber Soup

262
Basil Tomato Chilled
Soup

264
Chilled Honeydew and
Cucumber Soup with
Coconut Milk

264
Persian Watermelon
Soup

266
Zesty Lemon Yogurt
and Berry Soup

268
Spiced Yogurt and
Cherry Soup

270
Mulled Wine and
Orange "Soup"

GARNISHES,
BACON,
GRAINS, AND
OTHER GOOD
FOODS

274
Delicious Pesto

276
Basil Parsley Gremolata
and Garam Masala
Spice Mixture

278
Homemade Tortilla
Chips

280
No-Cook Pickled
Onions

282
Crème Fraîche

282
Pan-Fried Croutons

284
Italian Beef Meatballs
and Chicken Meatballs

286
Herbed Dumplings

288
Marbled Spiced Tea
Eggs

290
Soy Ginger
Slow-Roasted Salmon

290
Everyday Mashed
Potatoes

292
Homemade Almond Milk

292
Basic Quinoa

(Soaked)

294
Soaked Brown Rice

296
White Rice

296
Ghee

298
Simple Homemade
Bacon

Introduction

With the dawn of humanity came soup. True, it was in a simplified form, but soup nevertheless. And as tribes turned into civilizations and nations, their soups evolved with them, transforming from simple, necessity-driven forms into art. Soup nourished native populations after a hunt, delighted the gourmet in ancient Rome, fed a family and servants from a pot kept over the fire continually during the medieval era, and stretched out bits of meat and vegetables during famines and the Great Depression. Soup has been with us since the earliest days of our culinary history. It has seen us in happy times, it has welcomed the harvest on our tables, delighted us at feasts, nourished us when ailing, served as a first food through the ages, and brought comfort in our last days.

Soups predate pots. Early forms of soup were made in animal hides placed over a fire or heated with hot stones. These hot stones could be dropped into pits in the ground or sand and filled with water, meat, and whatever else could be gathered or hunted. The hot stones brought the water to a boil, and within a few hours, there was a delicious hot soup—without a pot.

New methods and flavor combinations have been developed in the last 150 years, such as the Vietnamese noodle soup "pho," which is a flavorful beef or chicken soup that tantalizes the senses. Ancient flavor combinations have continued to evolve with us through the dance of produce, meat, and the work of our hands.

Along with the advent of factory-produced meat, lab-invented flavorings (such as the infamous MSG), and the technology and knowledge to can foods, our soup experience has changed. A mother might open a packet and add hot water to create a chicken noodle soup for an ailing child instead of stirring a soup in a stockpot. The memory of soup as nourishment for the body still lies deeply embedded in the human psyche, even when our form of soup no longer rebuilds a sick body. Restaurants often serve soups prepared in a factory or made of many canned products. Ethnic restaurants sometimes spike their soups with MSG, and let's not even mention the typical soup served at a grocery store deli. If all I had ever been served was a typical deli or restaurant soup, I'd probably believe I hated all soups.

But, thankfully, in my own early experience in the kitchen (when my skills were quite primitive), I discovered a love for homemade soup. During high school, I found several recipes that were delicious, frugal, and easy to make. My fingers grew weary of peeling butternut squash after hours of practicing piano, but that hot bowl of soup was always worth it in the end. While my own knowledge of cooking has grown substantially since those early years in my mother's kitchen, I still enjoy those first couple of soup recipes I created.

Today, as a mother on a budget, I appreciate the myriad of ways a soup can be made inexpensively. As the primary cook for my family, I'm grateful for the incredible nutrient-rich stores a stockpot can hold. As a lover of good food, I am thankful for the gourmet experience a homemade soup can provide. Soup can be rough and tumble, hearty fare, or as delicate as a breeze over lavender. We like to enjoy all sorts of soups and stews in my family, for there is certainly a recipe suitable for all occasions.

The aim of this book is simple. I wanted a soup and stew cookbook that was practical enough to use on a daily basis. I wanted it to contain plenty of simple-to-prepare soups that would bring warmth to my family's bellies and nourishment to their bones. I also wanted it to contain soups that were tempting enough for special occasions. I wanted my recipes to have new, fresh ideas, as well as historical soups that are still well worth making. In short, I wanted my book to be one that I planned on opening up myself on a daily basis. I figured I couldn't lose if I created a book that I would use regularly, because at least one person would be happy with my work!

But to make sure that this book didn't simply make me happy, I brought along more than one hundred volunteers to try my recipes, feed them to their families, and give me invaluable feedback. The vast majority of my recipe testers have no professional background but are just real people trying to nourish themselves and those around them. One of the questions I asked was, "Would you ever make this recipe again?" I wanted the majority of my recipes to be ones that they would want to enjoy over and over. I'm thankful for their faithful work on this book alongside me.

To help those with certain dietary restrictions, we've labeled recipes in this book with the following: Gluten-Free, Dairy-Free, Vegetarian-Friendly, Budget-Friendly, GAPS-Friendly, and Quick Recipe. Note that some recipes with these labels have vegetarian, gluten-free, or dairy-free options, so make sure you pay heed to those changes if they matter to you.

If you are a soup lover already, I hope this book adds more favorite recipes to your pile. If you're a new cook, I hope that the explanations, recipes, and pictorial guides help you find your feet in the kitchen. Soups are a great place to start. If you're a soup-reluctant eater, I hope you find some recipes you can enjoy. Most of all, it's my goal that these recipes bring enjoyment and nourishment into your weekly lives.

Appreciating Bones and the Stocks They Make

We like our meat battered, crumbed, seasoned, fried, and then presented. Most of us have completely lost touch with where it came from and how that animal was treated before it found its way to our plate. And we like it that way. At least, I know I did when I first started working with meat in the kitchen at the age of fifteen. I remember to this day having to handle a raw chicken breast for the first time and literally gagging as I touched it. I tried to handle it, look at it, and smell it as little as possible. My first experience certainly was just that—an experience!

Now, I handle not only raw chicken breast, but also beef bones, chicken feet, animal livers, and pork fatback on a regular basis with no problem. What happened to this animal-loving, queasy girl of yesterday? Have I become some animal Nazi, immune to the sight of blood? Far from it. The fact is that my love for animals is still strong. We had some egg-laying hens for a while, and when a coyote broke through and killed them, I cried over their broken bodies. While I have faced far greater personal tragedies in my life than the loss of a chicken, these hens had become pets of a sort, and my heart held affection and compassion for them in their last suffering hour.

Yet, when a friend found me in my kitchen adding chicken feet to a stockpot, she was taken aback. "That is just . . . too much for me!" she said. To her, the addition of bones, chicken feet, and whatnot was somehow disrespectful to the dead animal. In my opinion, if this animal is going to die to nourish my family, by golly, I'll get every piece of nutrition I can out of it! I don't want to waste that sacrifice.

I try my hardest to stretch our budget to buy chickens that were raised in a happy, healthy environment and killed humanely (I am sure that the chickens I eat suffered far less than my chickens so cruelly torn apart by wild animals). Not only did those chickens (or cows) have happy, healthy lives, but they also, in turn, nourished our family with better nutrition and less toxicity when compared to their factory-produced counterparts.

One way we show appreciation for the animals that die to feed us is by not wasting them. That is one reason it's an ethical practice to make your own soup stocks at home.

But that isn't all there is to appreciating bones.

Stocks made out of bones are a health food.

When you make a homemade stock out of chicken, beef, turkey, or other bones, you make a nourishing stock that is perhaps one of the healthiest food items you can feed to your family. This isn't simply about showing honor to the animal; this is about being smart nutritionally.

What's so special about stock? So many things that it's hard to list them all. Let's start with gelatin. This is one of the first differences I noticed when making my own chicken stock. While I was accustomed to thin and watery chicken stock, even when cold, my homemade chicken stock would gel up when refrigerated. "What is this strange Jell-O-like dish I have made?" I wondered. Well, that gelling effect was caused entirely by my stock's gelatin content, and there is a lot that's special about gelatin.

Gelatin is a rich source of proline, which new evidence demonstrates might be an essential amino acid. It is also an excellent source of glycine, crucial for many of our body's processes, including manufacturing glucose and the synthesis of hemoglobin, bile salts, and more. Glycine is vital for the body's normal forms of detoxification, and it aids digestion by enhancing gastric acid secretion (a lack of stomach acid is a chronic problem for many). It's also crucial for wound healing, as the body needs glycine to repair the body, and it's important for the proper growth of infants and young children. While the body can create its own glycine, there is evidence that a diet rich in it is beneficial.[1]

Stocks made with bones, such as chicken, lamb, or beef, are an excellent source of many minerals. Think of it this way: Bones need a variety of minerals and essential amino acids to be built. When you make a slow-simmering broth out of bones, you are gradually leeching out those minerals into a flavorful, easy-to-absorb form. We know that stock is especially rich in calcium, and one study showed that the longer a stock is cooked, the more calcium it contains. They also found that when you add vinegar to the cooking water, even more calcium is leeched into the stock. If you want strong bones and teeth, broth made out of slow-simmered bones may be part of the answer.[2]

Chicken soup is often given to the sick, and many cultures have proverbs praising the virtues of chicken soup in helping people with a cold or flu. It's called the "Jewish Penicillin," after all. This ancient wisdom is getting new traction as science starts to catch up. For example, one scientist found that homemade chicken stock inhibited the migration of neutrophils, which is the most common type of white blood cell. He theorized that this inhabitation helps reduce upper respiratory cold symptoms. A separate study found that chicken broth is the most effective in "increasing nasal mucus velocity." In other words, it helps to unclog a stuffy nose.[3]

The Gut and Psychology Syndrome (GAPS) diet by Dr. Natasha Campbell-McBride uses the healing power of stock in her diet that seeks to heal the gut. Homemade stock is eaten every day in her diet, and at every meal during the beginning stages. That's because homemade stock not only gives you excellent nutrition, but also helps to heal the gut.

Appreciating bones means appreciating the healing they can bring us. But I don't want to leave some of the vegetable broths completely out of this section. They have their own benefit. They are made using nutritious ingredients like cancer-fighting onions and garlic, immune-boosting mushrooms, and alkaline-forming carrots and other vegetables.

For an especially nutritious broth, make a simple one using stinging nettles, which is a wonder-food because of its abundant vitamins. Of course, you can make homemade chicken or beef stock with immune-boosting, nutrient-special vegetables like nettles too! Then, you can have the benefits of both. Just add a handful or two of vegetables to a pot of simmering stock.

Homemade Stocks are Delicious

We can't forget the last reason we should appreciate homemade stocks: They are absolutely delicious. Is it any wonder that the French built their cuisine around homemade stock? If you can make a simple homemade stock, you will have the base for many delicious dishes. Not only that, but I have found it an easy way to make meals. If you have a rich broth on hand, you only need a couple of vegetables and perhaps some noodles, potatoes, and protein to make a meal within minutes.

I often create soups using leftover grains and spare vegetables, which is an especially frugal and easy way to make soups. I love making my own broths, including vegetable, because they taste so wonderful, and that is one of the most important reasons we should appreciate them.

Why I Am a Traditional Cook

I consider myself a "traditionalist" when it comes to the kitchen. I use traditional ingredients and traditional methods, and I enjoy traditional recipes (or use traditional ingredients in new ways, which is an exciting, never-ending process of experimentation). This is a delicious way to live, but is it the healthiest?

It can be confusing to wade through all of the research as to which foods create the true "health" diet. I personally believe that part of the reason it's so confusing is that we all have unique genetic backgrounds, histories, and relationships with food. What is healthy for one person may not promote the best health for another. The foundation of a healthy diet lies in traditional ingredients that are nutrient dense, but the specifics of what constitutes a healthy diet vary widely.

Two men who have greatly influenced me are Dr. Weston A. Price, who lived at the beginning of the twentieth century when traditional foods were just starting to be replaced by refined factory foods, and Dr. Nicholas Gonzalez, who is building on Dr. Price's legacy and other voices before him and also breaking new ground of his own.

Introducing Dr. Weston A. Price

Dr. Weston A. Price was a dentist who lived from 1870 to 1948 when industrial foods were starting to spread like wildfire. Spurred on by the death of his son from a tooth infection and his own experience with tooth decay while eating a typical diet, as well as his subsequent healing when he ate food off the land while camping, he became intrigued by the question, "Why do teeth decay?"

That question led him to travel the world and compare people who were eating canned foods, jams, white sugar, white flour, and vegetable oil with those who ate traditional fare. His discoveries are very relevant and helpful to us today.

He observed and studied fourteen groups of healthy people around the world—from the United States to Switzerland to Peru to Africa. All of these groups ate very different diets, but they had more in common than you would think at first glance. The first observation he made was that people who ate their country's traditional foods were robust and healthy with wide jaws to support good teeth structure, very few to zero cavities, and a resistance to the common plagues of that time such as tuberculosis. Those who ate a lot of the new industrial foods like refined sugar, flour, and vegetable oils often had rampant tooth decay and little resistance to disease. He documented his findings with pictures and recorded the health of people's teeth and facial structure. The difference between the groups was often alarming.

While he documented a limited number of groups of people, he was able to pick up very distinct patterns in all fourteen of the robust people groups he studied. Despite their varied diets, the groups all had certain dietary principles in common. From his book *Nutrition and Physical Degeneration*, these are the main attributes of the various diets he found:

SWITZERLAND: Dark rye bread, homemade cheese and butter from grass-fed cows (with particular value placed on spring butter that was made when the grass grew rapidly), and generally one meat dish a week, as well as soups made from the leftover meat dish.

BRITISH ISLES: Oats, seafood, and produce.

MASAI TRIBE: Milk (often soured), blood from cattle during the dry season of milking, and meat.

MAORI: Shellfish, kelp, grubs, fern roots, and other produce and seafood.

PERU: Parched corn and beans, coca leaves, fish, fruits, and vegetables (among other food items depending on which group of isolated Peruvians he was with).

Everyone's menu varied somewhat, if not dramatically, yet all of these people had robust health. As we consider what it means to "eat well," it's important to remember that there isn't some regimented perfect diet that the whole planet should eat. It can be diverse.

How much nutritional value these traditional diets contained is a vital point. One aspect of Dr. Price's research was sending samples of the foods to labs to test their nutritional value. This is where we start seeing unity in the diverse diets. All of them were significantly higher in certain nutrients than the typical modern diet of his time.

While there were many nutrients to study, and their diets were probably higher in all nutrients across the board, Dr. Price especially noticed high levels of calcium, phosphorus, vitamins A and D, and something he called the "X factor" which is now thought to be vitamin K2. He believed that these vitamins and minerals worked in a synergy together to create a healthy diet. Even though the sources of these minerals and vitamins varied by culture, they were all high. In fact, the diets had typically two to five times more essential fatty acids, minerals, and water-soluble vitamins and ten times more of vitamins A and D than the modern diet.[4] It makes sense to mimic these high nutrient diets if we also want to have robust health. Dr. Price used calcium rich homemade stocks as an important facet in the nourishing diets he created to help the health of poverty stricken children since it was so nutritious.

As a final word about Dr. Price's research, I should note that he was most impressed with those who ate a high seafood diet, and that he was unable to find a people group with thriving health who survived solely on a vegan diet for more than a couple of generations.

Meet Dr. Gonzalez

Dr. Gonzalez has had incredible results treating cancer patients with alternative methods and care at his clinic in New York. One important part of his treatment is diet. Unlike alternative doctors in the past who had a one-size-fits-all diet, Dr. Gonzalez has found it vital that people eat a diet especially suited to them for healing. His healing protocols vary from nearly vegetarian diets to a diet close to that of the Eskimo with plenty of fat and protein. While, thankfully, most of us don't have to be on such a specific healing diet, the principle of different diets for different people holds true for healthy individuals as well.

One simple way that you can tell what works best for you is self-experimentation. Do you feel satisfied, and are you thriving when you eat a high-protein, low-carbohydrate diet? Or do you feel fatigued when you eat a low-carb diet? Eating what makes you thrive is important.

Dr. Gonzalez believes that part of the reason we thrive on different diets is because of our genetic background. He probably would question whether an Eskimo could rapidly change to the diet of the Peruvian and still feel great. We adapted to the foods in our area over hundreds, even thousands of years. This might be one reason why Native Americans have such alarmingly high rates of obesity and diabetes. Europeans and European Americans adapted, at least to a certain point, to foods such as wheat flour as it was slowly introduced and cultivated. But it was dumped on Native Americans rather suddenly in their history of traditional foods. Many tribes are starting to fight the modern epidemic of diabetes by going back to their traditional diets. We would be wise to follow their example.

You can read more about Dr. Gonzalez's research in Suzanne Somers's book, *Knockout: Interviews with Doctors Who Are Curing Cancer—and How to Prevent Getting It in the First Place.*

How Traditional Food Translates to Recipes in My Diet and This Book

While this book isn't trying to promote any exact formula for your diet, my recipes use "real food" or "traditional food." Eating this way is actually quite simple—quinoa, rice, legumes, a rainbow of produce, grass-fed beef, organic chicken (pastured when possible), lamb, and seafood. I avoid most modern oils that are low in omega-3s and/or highly processed oils like canola and soy. Instead, I use extra-virgin olive oil, coconut oil, homemade lard or tallow, and duck fat. As long as my ingredients are good, I don't worry too much about anything else. I use unrefined salt, and I salt dishes and soups to taste. I use enough fat to be able to properly sauté and brown ingredients as needed. No nonstick pans here! This philosophy greatly simplifies most things in the kitchen.

While I started this book with the intention of especially highlighting soups in which you can use nourishing homemade beef, chicken, and other "bone broths," I concluded that having vegetarian options would be valuable as well. I'm aware that some people thrive on an omnivorous diet on a regular basis but need a vegetarian diet for a period of healing or cleansing. Dr. Gonzalez convinced me that there are those who naturally thrive on a vegetarian or nearly vegetarian diet, at least for a period of time. So, I wanted this book to also be accessible to those people. For that reason, I played around with a variety of vegetable broths so that I could provide vegetarian and omnivorous eaters alike with a good substitute to meat stocks. I was pleased with the result of those experiments. I put together a group of testers willing to play around with my recipes to make them vegetarian friendly. Of course, some recipes were "naturally" vegetarian already.

What's with the Funny Directions for Soaking Grains in Your Recipes?

I think that the most unusual aspect of my recipes is my method of soaking, fermenting, or sprouting grains. This needs explanation. Consuming fermented grains is an ancient, worldwide practice that we only lost in more recent years. Methods vary widely from country to country, as do the grains and legumes used. Research has taken place in hundreds of studies demonstrating the possible benefits of some of these ancient practices. Examples of historical foods that are fermented include Japanese or Korean-fermented soy and rice pastes (such as miso), traditionally fermented grain porridges from Africa, American sourdough bread, or nixtamalized corn from Native Americans.

The Problem with Grains and Beans

Research has found that whole grains and legumes contain numerous "antinutrients." These substances prevent us from absorbing the full nutritional value of the grains or beans. The most widely researched is phytic acid (or phytate), which can block you from absorbing calcium, magnesium, iron, and zinc. It can also inhibit natural enzymes, which help you properly digest food. Phytate has been labeled by the World Health Organization as one of the main causes of anemia because of its ability to block the absorption of iron.

Phytic acid levels depend on the grain or legume, as well as the conditions in which that grain or legume was grown (even the weather during growing seasons can effect phytic acid levels), but all grains and legumes contain it to some degree. There is an enzyme called phytase that unlocks and neutralizes phytic acid, and in the kitchen I try to release phytase to do its business.

If you depend on a lot of grains and legumes for your daily nutritional needs, properly preparing them could be vital for your health. While some people break down phytic acid better in their digestive tracts than others, fermenting, "soaking," or sprouting your grains and legumes will help you jump-start that process.

Just as old methods of fermenting grains varied, so does current research, which uses different methods to reduce phytic acid. First, you should know that wheat, barley, and buckwheat naturally contain higher amounts of phytase, so you will have more success soaking them to reduce phytic acid. Grains low in phytase include corn, millet, and brown rice.

Many different studies have found that when you sprout grains or legumes, you raise phytase and substantially reduce phytic acid. Because sprouted grains are so high in phytase, researchers found that vigorously shaking the sprouted grains together with non-sprouted flour reduces the phytic acid in the non-sprouted flour. When fermenting, the common lactobacillus bacteria was found to not only reduce phytic acid, but also to contain the enzyme amylase that helps break down starch (which could, in turn, make the starch in your grains more digestible).

How do we recreate this in our kitchen? There are numerous ways.

SPROUTING

We can sprout our own legumes and grains or use sprouted flour. There are more and more sprouted grain and legume products on the market, so you don't necessarily have to do the work yourself. Using sprouted flour in baked goods is an easy way to make more nutritious food that is also more digestible. There are also sprouted grains (like brown rice or quinoa) and beans for sale in health food stores. Sprouting them yourself at home is a simple process of soaking the grains or legumes for eight hours and then rinsing and draining them every twelve hours or so until tiny sprouts start to grow. They can then be used in any recipe, including soups. You just need to make sure you start with a grain that hasn't been heat-processed, in which case it will never sprout.

SOAKING GRAINS

You can also soak grains in warm water with a live-bacteria addition such as yogurt, raw apple cider vinegar, kefir, kombucha, or other fermented food. The addition brings down the pH of the water, which is important because it helps to create an acidic environment in which phytase is best unlocked. Plus, with a live-culture addition, you are also starting a fermentation process, as that live bacteria starts working on breaking down the grain.

It's easy to see how this process can make the grain more digestible. I've talked to many people who have trouble digesting regular whole-grain products who can easily handle soaked grains. However, I've chosen not to add acidic, live cultures to my legume recipes in the book because it occasionally caused my legumes to take a very long time to cook. However, keep in mind that soaking beans with a live culture or sprouting them is the best method of reducing phytic acid in legumes.

WARMTH

When soaking grains, it's important to do so in a warm environment. During the summer months, this shouldn't be an issue. During the cold of winter, place your soaking grains in a warm room or place such as on top of the refrigerator. Warmth is important for rapidly breaking down antinutrients.

LENGTH OF TIME

The longer you soak or sprout a grain or legume, the more phytic acid and predigesting you will accomplish. You should note, however, that you shouldn't soak or ferment them too long. If you're in a particularly warm climate, soak or ferment a shorter amount of time, as you can end up with a very sour or moldy product. If you want to soak for long periods of time, rinse and replace the soaking liquid every twelve to twenty-four hours.

FERMENTING

Fermented breads, such as sourdough, are highly effective in reducing antinutrients. The art of baking with sourdough is beyond the scope of this book, but I encourage you to look into it. You can also often find traditionally made sourdough in stores and bakeries. Look for versions that contain no yeast in the ingredient list.

FRESHLY MILLED GRAINS

Freshly milled grains will contain much higher amounts of phytase, which is important for reducing phytic acid. After a grain is milled, it starts to lose phytase content, so it is best practice to use freshly milled grains when soaking or fermenting flours for baked goods.

Questions and Answers about Soaking Grains

I've tried to keep all of the soaking methods in this book simple since the primary thrust of the book is to make delicious soups using nourishing stocks and broths. If you'd rather not soak your grains, the recipes are easily adapted to non-soaking cooking times; you may just need to add more liquid to the recipe.

Q: Is it safe to leave grains soaking at room temperature?

A: I remember being a little nervous myself about leaving grains out to "soak" when I first started. We are so used to putting everything in the refrigerator, but leaving the grains out is perfectly safe. Just a few generations ago, our grandparents left oatmeal out to soak overnight before cooking it. No one thought anything of it. I have found, however, that in really warm weather, shorter soaking times are preferable. If you soak for too long, your grains could start to smell and taste strange. Never consume any soaked or fermented food that has molded or smells strange. If you are soaking for longer than twelve hours in really warm weather, drain and rinse the grains and add new water to the bowl to prevent mold and odors.

Q: I'm interested in learning more about this topic. What resources do you recommend?

A: I discuss the research side of this topic at this web address: www.thenourishinggourmet. com/2012/01/whats-the-fuss-about-soaking-grains-explanation-and-research-shared.html.[5]

Nourishing Traditions: The Cookbook That Challenges Politically Correct Nutrition and the Diet Dictocrats by Sally Fallon and Mary Enig is an excellent resource as well. I, and many other bloggers, share "soaked" grain recipes on a regular basis at www. thenourishinggourmet.com.

Q: Why do you use white rice in this book?

A: I have chosen to use white rice in some recipes. How can I do that when I'm into whole food? In the book, *Perfect Health Diet: Four Steps to Renewed Health, Youthful Vitality, and Long Life,* by Paul Jaminet and Shou-Ching Jaminet, I found the use of white rice very interesting. They point to an Italian study that found that brown rice contains phytin and other antinutrients that are believed to cause a poorer mineral balance. Granted, the brown rice wasn't fermented or soaked in the study, so it wasn't a fair comparison. But because brown rice is low in phytase, it is a harder grain to properly prepare for breaking down antinutrients. Plus, the authors point out that rice protein found in rice bran provokes an immune response, which could indicate toxicity. Many have chosen to call white rice a "safe starch" for this reason. If you use brown rice, consider following my instructions on page 294 for soaking it.

Ingredient Guide

These recipes were primarily tested with organic or better-than-organic ingredients. Pesticide residue is much higher, of course, in foods that are raised conventionally. Recent studies have found that children have much less pesticide residue in their bodies when eating an organic diet,[6] which is important since pesticides have long been linked to a variety of health issues, including ADHD.[7]

Produce

Organic foods can be expensive. If you're on a tight budget, try to buy organic for the produce on the "dirty dozen" list. These are the ones that are most contaminated with pesticides. According to the Environmental Working Group (EWG) for 2012, the list includes: apples, celery, sweet bell peppers, peaches, strawberries, imported nectarines, grapes, spinach, lettuce, cucumbers, domestic blueberries, and potatoes. (Also recommended by EWG to buy organic are green beans and kale/greens.)[8]

Beef

The majority of the beef I use is 100 percent grass-fed. I buy from a "cow share" from local farmers and keep it in my freezer. Grass-fed beef has a much higher omega-3 fatty acid content and also contains CLA (conjugated linoleic acid). CLA has shown in studies to have an anticancer effect, reduce fat, build lean muscle, and promote anti-atherosclerotic activity, which may prevent heart disease. For these reasons, some have even begun to call grass-fed beef a "super food." Grass-fed dairy is also much higher in nutrients, so I try to find grass-fed dairy whenever I can. I make this possible financially by buying in bulk directly from a farmer once a year.

> Using the highest quality ingredients you can afford always pays off with better health and taste.

Poultry and Eggs

The very best poultry and eggs are bought from local farmers who pasture their chickens, allowing them to eat plenty of bugs and greens from their natural environment. The chicken will have a richer, fuller flavor, as well as provide a purer product. The eggs will also have rich, golden yolks. If pastured chicken is not available, organic, free-range chicken and chicken eggs are the next best choice. You will notice that I use a lot of drumsticks in my recipes. This is because I'm able to find organic, free-range chicken drumsticks at Trader Joe's for a good price. While not the best-of-the-best (which would be pastured chicken), they do provide a high-quality product without the need to spend a lot of money.

Unrefined Salt

Salt is a very important part of a delicious soup. The most common cause of a flavorless homemade soup is lack of salt. It helps bring out the flavor of soups and stews. Plus, when using an unrefined salt, you get trace minerals and avoid the bleaching and refining process most salt goes through. There are a lot of excellent options. Look at my resource page at the end of the book for specific recommendations.

Look for a salt that hasn't been refined and bleached, such as unrefined sea salts. Andes pink salt, Hawaiian red salt, and Himalayan crystal salt are good options. One unique salt that you can use in soups is a naturally smoked sea salt. It adds a fabulous smoky flavor to any dish.

Guide to Fats and Oils

I've done something a little unusual in this book by listing "fat of choice" in most of the recipes. I've done this simply because there are a variety of fats and oils that can easily be used.

Here is a guide to some of the traditional fats and oils (with a couple of new oils on the market) to help you navigate which fat to choose. Check out the resource page at the back of the book for specific brand recommendations.

Coconut Oil

Unrefined or raw virgin coconut oil has a faint to strong coconut scent and flavor. It is solid at cold temperatures and liquid when warm. Its smoke point is 350F/177C. It contains high lauric acid levels, which have antifungal, antibacterial, and antivirus properties. Refined coconut oil has no taste and has a high smoke point of 450F/232C.

What to buy: Coconut oil that is made with organic coconuts and left in its raw, unrefined state or a refined coconut oil that is expeller-pressed. Don't buy hydrogenated coconut oil or copra (or RBC) coconut oil that has been bleached and deodorized.

How to use: Use virgin coconut-oil at low to medium heat. Expeller-pressed coconut oil is suitable for high-heat projects including frying.

Ghee and Butter

Ghee is a clarified butter that is highly concentrated because the milk proteins have been removed, which means it doesn't burn at a low temperature and leaves a very rich fat behind. Ghee's smoke point is 485F/251C. Learn how to make it yourself on page 296.

What to buy: Try to buy organic butter to avoid the high pesticide amounts in conventional butters. Look especially for brands that are from grass-fed cows.

How to use: Use butters when making a roux, to finish a soup, or to spread on a piece of bread. Ghee is suitable for use in higher heat applications, such as sautéing.

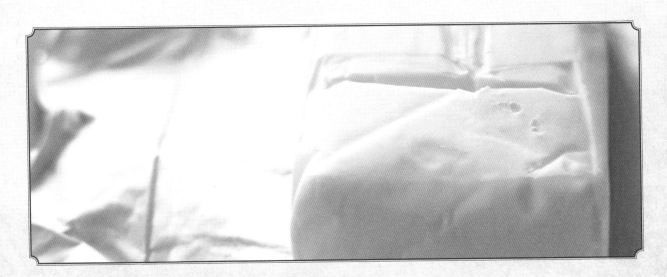

Tallow and Lard

Beef and pork fat have only been recently overthrown for oils rich in omega-6 such as canola and other vegetable oils. However, when made with quality ingredients, they can be a wonderful part of a nourishing diet.

What to buy: It's important that you don't buy lard from the typical grocery store, as it is almost always hydrogenated. Some small farmers make their own when butchering their animals. Otherwise, you can buy grass-fed or pastured beef suet to make your own tallow or leaf lard to render. Directions for rendering your own lard are at this web address: www.thenourishinggourmet.com/2009/04/how-to-render-lard.html.[9]

How to use: Both tallow and lard are heat stable, so they make excellent choices for sautéing or frying foods. Lard has a smoke point of 370F/188C, while tallow has a smoke point of 420F/220C.

Extra-Virgin Olive Oil

Extra-virgin olive oil can be bright green with a bite or yellow in color and warm and gentle in flavor. The most important aspect to consider is the source of your olive oil, as many extra-virgin olive oils have been secretly diluted with inferior oils. Look at my resource guide at the end of the book for brands I buy and recommend.

What to buy: Local, American-based olive oil from farmers you trust or farm-direct olive oils.

How to use: Olive oil is best used in cold applications or in drizzling over a bowl of soup, as its more delicate structure can be damaged through heat (although some Mediterranean countries use it as an all-purpose cooking oil). There is conflicting information as to olive oil's smoke point. It depends somewhat on the specific oil and whether or not it has been filtered.

Sesame Seed Oil and Toasted Sesame Seed Oil

Sesame seed oil has been used since ancient times. While it contains a higher amount of omega-6 fatty acids, it isn't highly processed like many modern vegetable oils. Because of the high amount of antioxidants in sesame oil, it isn't prone to rancidity and is a good source of vitamin E. Toasted sesame oil is a flavorful, more fragile oil that is used to season foods with its toasty flavor. It's wonderful in Asian foods.

What to buy: Unrefined sesame oil, expeller-pressed sesame oil, or high-quality toasted sesame seed oil that is stored in a dark container.

How to use: Unrefined sesame oil has a smoke point of 350F/177C, and expeller-pressed is slightly higher. Use it to sauté foods. Don't cook with toasted sesame oil.

Macadamia Oil

A newer oil that is especially popular in Australian cuisine. It has a long shelf life, a high smoke point of 410F/210C, and a mild, nutty flavor.

What to buy: Unrefined, macadamia oil.

How to use: Use it like you would other heat-safe oils when sautéing or even frying.

Kitchen Tools

You can make wonderful soups with the most simple and basic of tools. If you have a large pot, a wooden spoon, a decent knife (even a cheap knife), and a cutting board, you can make the majority of recipes in this book. Buying a decent stainless steel stockpot will suffice. An enamel-covered pot, such as the famous Le Creuset brand, is a step up. When working with enamel-covered cast iron, never use above medium heat unless you are bringing the liquid to a boil.

When making your own stocks, you will need a way of straining them. I bought a very inexpensive RSVP Endurance Wide Rim Mesh Basket with a three-quart capacity, and I love it! It can be used to strain stocks, rinse soaked grains, rinse fruits, and also acts like a vegetable steamer. I use it every day. You can buy it on Amazon.com.

I almost hate to admit it, but I have been using a very inexpensive knife as my chopping knife of choice for the last two years. We lost my high-quality knife while on vacation (don't bring your kitchen knives on vacation), and with a tight budget, I couldn't replace it right away. I ended up with a Japanese-style Pure Komachi Santoku Knife. It is super-sharp and is a marvel. It isn't a forever knife, and it's much lighter than a high-quality one (which is a disadvantage), but there is no reason to chop with inferior knives when you can have such a sharp, durable one for so little. Having a sharp knife makes all the difference when working in the kitchen on a daily basis.

My other favorite-of-favorite-tools is my KitchenAid Immersion Blender. I've had mine for years now and have used it over and over again (and it is still holding up very well). It's very convenient for puréeing a soup right in your pot. You will notice that I especially like to purée vegetable soups. It's a great way to get children (and adults) to enjoy vegetables.

You also may find it helpful to have a slow cooker for making stock or cooking soups. I recommend the Hamilton Beach brand because it has a lead-free crock. I own a simple, inexpensive eight-quart model that I use frequently. It also works well for the continuous method of stock making (see page 42).

Other items in my kitchen include a large food processor and blender. Any quality brand will work just fine.

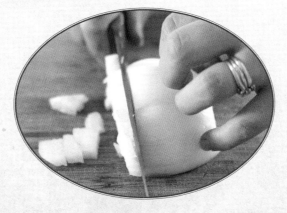

Basic Techniques and Instructions

Until recently, the Japanese use of "umami" to describe a certain flavor was considered an oddity of Japanese cuisine. Umami can be translated to mean "delicious" or "pleasant savory taste," and this delicious factor was separate from the "basic tastes" of salty, sour, sweet, and bitter. It turns out that they were on to something because science has proven them right. We actually have a specific receptor for umami on our tongues! When those receptors are titillated by umami, we think the food is "delicious."

So what is umami? A Japanese chemist by the name of Kikunae Ikeda wondered why a broth his wife made out of seaweed tasted so great even though it wasn't salty, sour, sweet, or bitter. He noticed this same flavor in asparagus, tomatoes, cheese, and meat. For years, he worked at discovering what element made food have this delicious flavor until he finally isolated it to a specific amino acid, L-glutamate. He went on to create a stable form of L-glutamate called monosodium glutamate, otherwise known as MSG. It was a revolution, as it added that "delicious" factor with a sprinkle of white powder. But as always seems to happen when we shortchange traditional methods, MSG dragged down the quality of food.

MSG is often used to mask a poorly made dish. If you'd rather not do the work or let a pot simmer gently on the stove for a couple of hours, you can get the instant gratification of that umami factor by simply using MSG or a product containing MSG. Little chicken noodle soup packets to which you add hot water are high in MSG because that's what makes your brain

think it tastes good. Asian ramen noodles are infamous for MSG levels, and canned cream of vegetable or chicken soups also contain high amounts. Besides lowering our food quality, MSG gives many people terrible headaches.

MSG gives us what our tongues know to be good, but in an unnatural form. Our L-glutamate receptors reward us when we taste food that contains it. However, I find that it can be overly rewarding. When I eat a big bowl of pho soup at the typical Vietnamese restaurant, I find the first few bites almost overwhelmingly delicious. It's because of all that MSG. But I can almost never finish a bowl because it just ends up being overwhelming after half of it is gone. When I make it at home, I delight from the first bite to the last because I use natural L-glutamate that is well balanced with the other flavors and profiles.

Besides that, MSG has been controversial since it appeared on the market. It's considered a neurotoxin by many and is linked to many mental and physical disorders. I'd much rather get my L-glutamate in its natural, traditional form.

So, how do you make soups and stews delicious with natural umami factor?
Here is a short list of ingredients that have umami:

STOCKS: Beef and chicken have plenty of umami, especially when made with bones that have been roasted, but are also rounded out with other flavor profiles. The Japanese and Korean broths using dried fish and seaweed are considered to be a more straightforward umami flavor.

AGED CHEESE: Parmesan is one of the most concentrated forms of L-glutamate foods.

CURED MEATS: As meat cures, it increases in L-glutamate content.

BROWNED MEATS: When you brown meat before stewing it or roast bones before making it into stock, you increase the L-glutamate content, which is why it tastes so good.

SOY SAUCE AND FISH SAUCE: Both are potent in L-glutamate.

RIPE TOMATOES: Tomatoes are also especially rich in L-glutamate.

Other foods high in L-glutamate include: fish and seafood, mushrooms, and green tea.

When a soup isn't flavorful enough, adding bacon, tomatoes, topping it with Parmesan or soy sauce, or using a rich broth will all add the umami factor that people crave. When you make a pho stock, you don't brown the bones, however. Instead, use fish sauce, which adds umami in concentrated form. I should also mention that soups that aren't flavorful enough are often not salted adequately.

Auguste Escoffier, one of the most important figures in modern French cuisine, was a master at creating a stock rich in flavor. He was, in fact, supercharging his stock with L-glutamate. His brown stock starts with roasted bones. He sautés his vegetables for the stock, then adds water along with the bones, pork rinds, herbs, and a clove of garlic. After the broth simmers for twelve hours, he browns beef scraps, deglazes the pan (capturing all of that flavor rich in L-glutamate), and adds that to the stock. I don't use all of these steps when making a stock, as I find them unnecessary for a beautiful broth. However, if you'd like to make an especially rich, umami stock, performing these extra steps will certainly up your flavor profile.

*P*reparing vegetables for a soup isn't hard, but it's helpful to know some general guidelines. Here are some basic instructions for preparing some of the common vegetables used in the recipes in this book.

Chopping an Onion

1. First, cut off the root end of the onion (try to cut the least amount off along with the root).

2. Cut the onion in half.

3. Peel both halves of the onion.

4. Slice the onion sideways once or twice, depending on how fine you want to chop your onion, and depending on the size of the onion. Cut almost all the way to the root end, but leave the onion intact, connected at the root.

5. Slice the onion halves top to bottom in ¼-inch/.6-cm slices.

6. Chop the onion toward the root end.

7. Finished Product.

Mincing Garlic

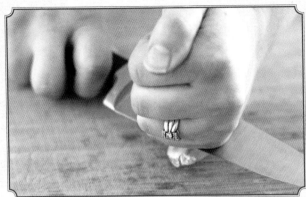

1. Put the flat side of the knife on the garlic clove. Using your fist, give it a hard and firm rap.

2. Peel the loosened garlic.

3. Cut the garlic sideways, once or twice (carefully).

4. Thinly slice the garlic, leaving the slices attached at the end.

5. Finely chop the garlic.

Slicing and Dicing Celery

Slice

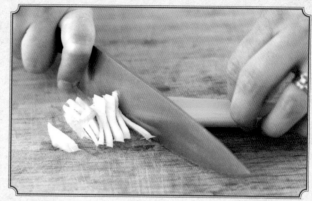

1. Cut the end off of the celery.

2. To slice, turn the knife at a slight diagonal and slice thin or thickly, depending on what you need.

Dice

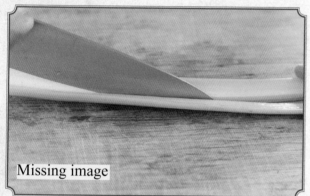

Missing image

1. To dice, cut the celery in half.

2. Cut each half in half again.

3. Gather the quarters together and chop.

Slicing and Dicing a Carrot

Slice

1. Cut off both ends of a peeled carrot.

2. Turn the knife at a slight diagonal and thinly or thickly slice, depending on your recipe.

Dice

1. For dicing, cut the carrot in half.

2. Cut each half in half again.

3. Gather the quarters together and chop.

Dicing a Potato

1. Cut the potato in half.

2. Slice each potato in half sideways (or twice, if using a large potato).

3. Slice each half in half again lengthwise into ½-inch/1.2-cm (or desired size) slices.

4. Chop the potato into ½-inch/1.2-cm cubes. (Note: When cubing for a stew, use the same method, but cut into larger pieces.)

Slicing Leeks

1. Cut off the dark green top of the leek, leaving about 1-inch/2.5-cm along with the lighter green/white part. (Save and use in stocks or broths.)

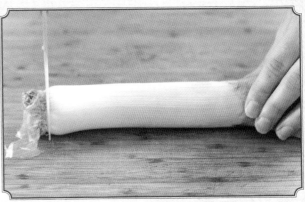

2. Cut off the root end as close to the roots as you can, leaving the leek still connected.

3. Shave off the dark green outer leaves at the top of the leek, leaving the inner core. (Optional)

4. Slice down the middle of the leek, leaving it attached at the root end.

5. Rinse the leek under running water, separating each layer to rinse well.

6. Slice into ¼-inch/1.2-cm pieces.

How to Sauté

1. Prepare your desired vegetables.

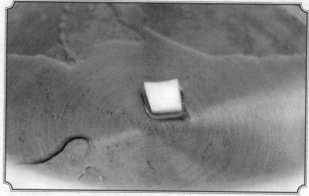

2. Add fat to the pan over medium or medium-high heat. Add one piece of onion. When the onion starts to sizzle, add the rest of the vegetables. Never allow any fat to smoke.

3. Sprinkle the vegetables generously with salt. (I don't add salt when using uncooked beans in a soup.)

4. Stir as needed to avoid browning or burning the vegetables.

5. When the vegetables are soft and the onions turn translucent, they are done (about five to seven minutes).

Carrot and Zucchini Noodles

1. This method works for zucchini as well. Place a peeled carrot on a cutting board. Run a vegetable peeler along the carrot from top to bottom, creating thin noodles until you reach the middle of the carrot.

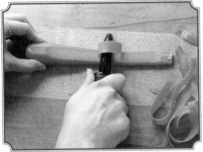

2. Turn the carrot over and do the same on the other side.

3. You will be left with a thin strip of carrot. Save it for use in a broth.

4. You can use the carrot noodles as is.

5. To make thin noodles, lay five carrot strips in a pile.

6. Cut the noodles into thin strips.

7. Finished product.

I also like to make vegetable noodles with a spiralizer. I use the World Cuisine Plastic Spiral Vegetable Slicer. Here is the method using zucchini. The method is the same for carrots or your vegetable of choice.

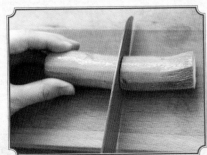

1. Cut a medium zucchini into 3-inch/7-cm pieces. Make sure to cut the edges flat.

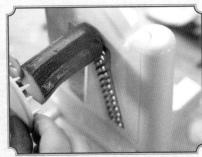

2. Center the zucchini on the machine using the smallest blade.

3. Exert gentle pressure sideways, turning the handle to make the noodles.

Homemade Sprouted Noodle Method

It's quite easy to make basic noodles with sprouted flour or otherwise.

1. In a bowl, combine one large egg with 1 cup/135 grams of flour (sprouted wheat, spelt, unbleached white flour, or a combination of white and sprouted flour). If the dough is very dry, add a tablespoon or less of water. Knead the dough on a clean counter until it becomes firm and not so sticky. Cover it with a towel and let it rest for twenty minutes.

2. Cut the dough in half and gently flatten one half with the palm of your hand.

3. Roll out the dough on a floured surface until it is very thin.

4. Cut the dough into thin strips using a sharp knife or pizza cutter.

5. Cook the noodles for about five minutes in salted, boiling water or until quite soft. Drain and serve right away.

Shelling Fresh Fava Beans

1. Place a large pot of water on the stove to boil and salt it well. Grab the stem end of each fava bean and snap it off, leaving the thin, thready piece of the bean (the "string") that connects to the middle of the fava bean in place.

2. Pull the string of the fava bean right down the middle of the bean, removing it and opening up the pod.

3. Use your fingers to open up the pod, if necessary, and remove the bean. Repeat with the rest of the pods.

4. Drop all of the fava beans into the pot of boiling water and boil for one minute. Meanwhile, set up a large bowl of cold water with ice.

5. Drain the fava beans, or remove them with a spider spoon, placing them in the cold water.

6. Once the beans are completely cooled, shell them again. There is a thin shell on the beans that is easily removed once they have been blanched.

7. Fava beans after all steps of the process.

Stocks, Broths, and Simple Soups

Stock is more than the backdrop to your soup's prima donna ingredients. The broth is the essence of your soup. My goal is to make the broth so scrumptious that I don't mind eating it plain, adorned only with salt. This holds true for meat and vegetable broths.

Nevertheless, there is no one right way to make stock. It can be made with carefully selected ratios of bones to meat to vegetables to water, or it can be made with scraps saved from other cooking projects. I've made 101 variations, with the vast majority of them working out quite well. Broth is very forgiving, so use the following recipes as guidelines to kick-start your own experimentations.

While the terms "broth" and "stock" are interchangeable, I generally use stock to designate a broth made out of bones, and broth for my vegetable broths.

Here are some tips with regard to stocks and broths

If you're accustomed to using store-bought broths, be aware that they are salted well. You may find yourself amazed at how much salt you need to add to homemade stock to make it taste right. Stock is thirsty for salt. The absolute number one reason a broth or soup tastes bland is because it is under-salted. For a fairly salty stock, use one teaspoon of salt to each quart of stock/broth.

* * *

You can make a very inexpensive stock by saving chicken bones from drumsticks, a chicken carcass, and vegetable scraps such as carrot peelings, mushroom stems, and even potato peels. Your exact results will vary depending on your ingredients, but I've used this method with great success. To ensure a rich stock, you can always add a couple of inexpensive raw drumsticks or chicken feet, which are also cheap but incredibly rich in flavor.

* * *

Avoid adding strong-flavored vegetables such as beet greens or meat that is beginning to sour. Dominant flavors from strong vegetables can overpower a whole pot of stock, and if your meat is starting to turn, it will make a bad-tasting and smelly broth.

* * *

A stock may not "gel" if it doesn't contain enough gelatin. This can be caused by a variety of things. The most common is simply adding too much water, which dilutes the gelatin. Pastured and true free-range chicken may make a more flavorful and gelatin-rich broth. Adding chicken feet will definitely increase gelatin content, but don't worry about it too much. Your stock will still taste great and be nutritious, even if it doesn't turn into a mass of gelatin in the refrigerator.

If your stock tastes bitter, the most common cause is that it was simmered for too long. I have found that twenty-four hours is the maximum time to simmer a chicken stock before I start tasting a slightly "off" flavor. My beef stocks can simmer up to forty-eight hours before I start to taste the same type of bitterness. If you add onion peels to your broth, beware that you don't cook them too long, as they also get bitter when cooked for longer periods of time.

* * *

The addition of apple cider vinegar in stocks creates a more acidic environment, which, when coupled with a long cooking time, allows the most minerals to be leeched from the bones. It does create a slightly more tart broth, but I love this taste. If you dislike the taste, there is no harm in omitting it.

* * *

It can be difficult to find fish bones. Many grocery stores no longer have experienced employees able to cut up a fish, since most fish comes pre-filleted. This means no fish bones. Look for specialty, high-end fish markets where they still buy whole fish and cut them up on the premises. If they are customer friendly (and know that you are also willing to buy fish from them), they should be willing to save the bones for you for free or for a minimal charge. You may also be able to find fish bones at Asian markets, but make sure you trust their fish sources. I have found it much harder to find fish bones in the suburbs than in the city. I was finally able to get some from a local high-end grocery store, but they only had whole cod when it was running, which is a short period of time every year. They saved me a huge bag of cod bones, which I made into pots and

pots of broth for freezing. When you can't find fish bones to make fish broth, you can make anchovy broth or substitute chicken stock in most recipes.

* * *

If you can, buy beef bones directly from a butcher; you can often even get them for free! When I buy my cow share, I ask for all of the bones they are willing to give me. Otherwise, I'm able to special-order knucklebones, marrowbones, oxtail, and whatever else I need from higher-end health food or specialty stores.

* * *

Stocks will last about five days refrigerated. If you'd like to extend that time, you can bring the stock to a boil every five days and refrigerate it for another five days. You can continue this method of reboiling the stock and refrigerating it for another five days indefinitely. Vegetable broths will last five days refrigerated. I haven't tried the reboiling method with them, although I imagine the principle would work the same.

Making Stock in a Slow Cooker, Reusing Bones, and the Continual Stock Method

Using a slow cooker can make things so much simpler when making bone stocks. The one issue is size. Even the largest slow cookers aren't as big as some of the stockpots you can purchase, but they provide an easy way to make stocks anytime. During the heat of summer they're especially helpful because they don't heat up your kitchen.

Any of the stock or broth recipes in this book can easily be adapted to the slow cooker. If you're roasting bones or vegetables, do that step first and then transfer them to the slow cooker.

I use a Hamilton Beach slow cooker since they're supposed to be free of lead. As you are cooking for long periods of time, I think it's especially helpful to have a lead-free crock. I bought an inexpensive, basic eight-quart model. I turn it on high for a couple of hours or until the broth simmers. Then, I turn it on low for the remainder of the cooking time.

Did you know that there is a way to reuse your chicken, lamb, turkey, and beef bones? Amanda Rose, Ph.D., author of the excellent book, Rebuild from Depression: A Nutrient Guide Including Depression in Pregnancy and Postpartum, wrote a guest post for my blog in which she gave tips for making frugal stocks. One of her tips was reusing bones over and over again to make subsequent pots of stock. You can do this in either a slow cooker or a stockpot.

First Method

Place the roasted beef or lamb bones, leftover chicken or turkey carcass, whole raw chicken, or chicken/turkey pieces in a slow cooker or pot. Add your desired vegetables (such as onions, carrots, celery), peppercorns, a couple of bay leaves, and apple cider vinegar and cover them with water. Simmer gently in a stockpot, or keep the slow cooker on low. After about twelve hours, strain the broth through a fine sieve. Refrigerate the broth and return the bones to the stockpot or slow cooker. Cover them with water again and repeat the process. I have found that chicken bones can make a flavorful stock up to three times. Beef can make broth five times, although it depends on what type of beef bones you use. (Amanda Rose mentioned that she got twelve batches from an especially well-suited beef bone called "beef feet.") I would only make two batches from fish bones.

Second Method

Place roasted beef or lamb bones, leftover chicken or turkey carcass, whole raw chicken, or chicken/turkey pieces in a slow cooker or pot. Add your desired vegetables or vegetable scraps (such as onion, carrots, celery), peppercorns, a couple of bay leaves, apple cider vinegar and cover them with water. After about twelve hours, you can strain the amount of stock you need through a fine sieve and replace the liquid taken out of the slow cooker or pot with more water. With this method, you just take what you need but never have to strain and restart the whole batch. The only disadvantage to this method is that your broth may become bitter if you don't take out enough stock throughout the week. Remember that over-simmered broth will start to produce off flavors or bitterness. So, if you use this second method, make sure that you don't leave it on the heat for too long without removing a significant ratio of stock and replacing it with water.

Regardless of the method you use, you can ensure that subsequent batches of broth are flavorful by adding some new ingredients along with the old. For example, one or more chicken feet (or chicken drumsticks) added to the second or third batch of chicken broth gives the stock plenty of gelatin and flavor. You can also roast one single extra beef bone and add it to a subsequent batch of stock along with the older bones.

Eventually, you will find that your bones become so soft that they start to fall apart. This demonstrates that you have fully simmered all of the nutrients out of the bones. Discard them at this point.

Sometimes, I don't use any vegetables at all, as they make it a little more complicated to strain the stock. If you do, however, replace the vegetables in every other batch, if not every batch, that you make with the same bones. Keep in mind, the first batch will always be the most flavorful.

This is definitely a money-saver, and it has allowed me to make a lot of soup for very little cost.

Basic Chicken Stock

Yield Varies

I use chicken stock most often for its gentle flavor. It's well-suited for a wide variety of soups, and it's easy to find the ingredients to make it. I like to roast a whole chicken and use the carcass to make chicken stock once a week. But you can also save any leftover drumsticks or other chicken bones in a bag in the freezer until you have a couple pounds' worth. You can also certainly use a raw whole chicken in place of the bones and drumsticks. It's hard to go wrong with chicken broth.

1 chicken carcass (or a bag of drumstick bones from the freezer)

1–2 pounds/450 to 900 grams raw drumsticks or chicken legs (I keep mine ready and frozen in the freezer)

3–5 chicken feet, optional (I also keep these frozen in the freezer)

Gizzards from the cavity of the chicken, optional

4 carrots, scrubbed, cut into 3-inch/7.6-cm pieces

4 celery sticks, washed, cut into 3-inch/7.6-cm pieces

1 onion, peeled, cut in half

1 bay leaf

15 peppercorns

Handful thyme sprigs, optional

2–4 tablespoons raw apple cider vinegar, optional

1. Place all of the ingredients into a large stockpot and cover them with filtered water up to 1–2 inches above the top of the ingredients. (If you are using vinegar and want to draw out more of the calcium from the bones, let the ingredients sit in the water for an hour at room temperature.)

2. Bring the stock to a low simmer over high heat. Then, turn the heat to low and cover. Never boil stock.

3. If you'd like moist and flavorful chicken meat to add to a soup, take out the drumsticks after 30 minutes, and let them cool. Remove the skin, shred the meat, and place it in the refrigerator. Return the bones to the pot.

4. Keep the stock at a very low simmer for at least three hours and up to 24 hours, skimming any foam that may rise to the top. The longer you simmer the stock, the more flavor and minerals will leach out into the water. Twelve hours works well; longer than 24 hours may cause the stock to become bitter and too dark.

5. When the stock is done, cool it slightly and strain it through a fine sieve or colander into a heat-safe bowl or other pot. For a clear stock, use cheesecloth or a coffee filter in the sieve. You can skim fat from the surface of the warm broth with a spoon (or a fat-skimming ladle) or chill the stock and scoop off the congealed fat from the surface.

Extra-Rich Chicken Broth

Replace the chicken carcass and drumsticks with one 3- to 5-pound whole chicken or raw chicken pieces. After simmering for 1 hour remove the chicken and cool. When cool enough to handle, remove the skin and shred all of the chicken meat. Save it to use in soups, to make chicken salad sandwiches, or to add to a variety of dishes. Add the bones back to the stock and continue cooking.

GLUTEN-FREE
Grain-free
GAPS-friendly
DAIRY-FREE
Budget-Friendly

Chicken Feet Stock

8–10 cups/1.8–2.3 liters

46

I used to be very squeamish about handling any type of raw meat. I hated it. Now, I easily make this stock with chicken feet. Nothing gets more of a reaction from my American friends than telling them I use chicken feet in my cooking (my Asian friends think it's great). It seems like a barbaric practice to some. But I tell them, "I cried when my egg-laying hens got killed by a coyote. I respect the animals that die to feed us, and I don't take that lightly. Using all usable parts of the animal is a respectful, non-wasting practice that this animal-loving carnivore strives to do." The thing about chicken feet is that they make a lovely, nutritious stock. It will be full of healthy gelatin and will make a stock that gels up dramatically. Chicken Feet Stock also cooks more quickly than bone broths. You can buy them from local farmers (best source) or from Asian supermarkets. If the chicken feet have a yellowish skin on them, read the preparation directions below.

1 pound/450 grams chicken feet (about 10 feet)

2 carrots, scrubbed, cut in half

2 celery sticks, cut in half

1 onion, peeled and quartered

3 garlic cloves, peeled

10–15 black peppercorns

2–4 tablespoons raw apple cider vinegar

Handful fresh thyme or 1 teaspoon dried thyme

10 cups/2.4 liters filtered water

1. Place all of the ingredients in a large pot and bring the stock to a boil. Turn down the heat and skim off any foam that rises to the surface.

2. Simmer gently for 3–12 hours.

3. Strain the stock well through a fine sieve or colander into a heat-safe bowl or pot. For a clear stock, use cheesecloth or a coffee filter in the sieve. You can skim fat from the surface of the warm broth with a spoon (or a fat-skimming ladle) or chill the stock and scoop off the congealed fat from the surface.

4. Use the stock right away, refrigerate it up to five days, or freeze it.

Directions for Skinning Chicken Feet

You won't need to do this step with most chicken feet bought in a store, but you may want to if you bought the feet directly from a farmer or butcher. This step is absolutely necessary for dishes where you plan on eating the meat from the chicken feet, however, some skip it when simply making stock. All you need is a pot with boiling water.

Bring a large pot of water to a boil. Drop in the chicken feet and simmer for a couple of minutes. Rinse the chicken feet to cool them. Starting at the opposite side of the claw, peel off the skin. You can also chop off the claws, but it's an unnecessary step for chicken feet used for making stock.

GLUTEN-FREE
Grain-free
GAPS-friendly
DAIRY-FREE
Budget-Friendly

Turkey Stock

Yield Varies

48

Turkey stock deserves to be made more than once a year. I love how flavorful it is. While it's definitely more assertive than chicken stock, you can easily change many of the chicken recipes in this cookbook to a turkey soup by using turkey meat and turkey stock. You can also make turkey stock with a slightly lighter flavor if you use raw turkey meat, such as turkey drumsticks, thighs, wings, or necks.

1 turkey carcass

4 carrots, scrubbed, cut into 3-inch/7.6-cm pieces

4 celery sticks, washed, cut into 3-inch/7.6-cm pieces

1 onion, peeled, cut in half

2 bay leaves, optional

15 peppercorns

Handful thyme sprigs, optional

2–4 tablespoons raw apple cider vinegar, optional

1. Place all of the ingredients into a large stockpot and cover them with filtered water up to 1–2 inches above the top of the ingredients. (If you're using the vinegar and want to draw out more of the calcium from the bones, let the stock sit for an hour at room temperature.)

2. Bring the stock to a low simmer over high heat. Then turn the heat to low and skim off any foam.

3. Keep the stock at a very low simmer for at least three hours and up to 24 hours, periodically skimming any foam that may rise to the top. The longer you simmer the stock, the more flavor and minerals will leach out into the water. Twelve hours works well; longer than 24 hours may cause the stock to become bitter and too dark.

4. When the stock is done, cool it slightly and strain it through a fine sieve or colander into a heat-safe bowl or other pot. For a clear stock, place cheesecloth or a coffee filter in the sieve. You can skim fat from the surface of the warm broth with a spoon (or a fat-skimming ladle) or chill the stock and scoop off the congealed fat from the surface.

49

GLUTEN-FREE
Grain-free
GAPS-friendly
Budget-Friendly

Beef Stock

Yield Varies

It took me a while to find a source of beef bones, but once I had them in my freezer, I found that beef stock is both easy and inexpensive. I get my bones directly from a farmer through a "cow share." You can even get bones free from many farmers. When I run out of those bones, I buy them from a local higher-end store. They sometimes have them in stock and are willing to special order them for me as well. I find that knucklebones are by far the cheapest bone to make into broth. Adding bones that are specifically designated as "soup bones" will add richness to your stock, but knucklebones make a delicious stock by themselves. The roasting adds a lot of flavor, so don't skip it.

3–5 pounds/1.4–2.3 kilograms beef bones (marrow, knuckle, oxtail, "soup bones," etc.; ask your butcher to cut them to expose the marrow, if possible)	2 carrots, peeled, cut in half 2 celery sticks, cut in half 3 garlic cloves, peeled 1 onion, peeled and quartered	2 bay leaves 1 tablespoon black peppercorns 2–4 tablespoons raw apple cider vinegar, optional

1. Preheat the oven to 400F/205C. Place all of the ingredients except the bay leaves, peppercorns, and apple cider vinegar in an ovenproof pot. If you'd like, melt some ghee or fat of your choice (see page 23) to drizzle over the bones and vegetables for better roasting. (I usually skip the fat, as enough is released from the bones themselves.)

2. Cook for 30–45 minutes, flipping the bones and vegetables if needed, until they begin to brown. Remove the pot from the oven and cool until warm.

3. Add water to the pot until the water reaches 1–2 inches above the bones.

4. Add the bay leaves, peppercorns, and apple cider vinegar (if using).

5. Leave the pot for one hour at room temperature to jump-start the apple cider vinegar action on the bones. (If you are not using vinegar, skip this step.)

6. Place the pot on the stove over low heat and bring the stock to a low simmer. Skim off any foam that comes to the surface. Simmer on low for 12–48 hours (three hours is the minimum for taste, but nutrition and depth of flavor will improve at the longer times). Reuse the bones as desired according to the instructions on page 42.

7. When the stock is done, strain it through a fine sieve or colander into a heat-safe bowl. Cool it and place it in the refrigerator. For a clear stock, use cheesecloth or a coffee filter in the sieve. You can skim fat from the surface of the warm broth with a spoon (or a fat-skimming ladle) or chill the stock and scoop off the congealed fat from the surface.

GLUTEN-FREE
Grain-free
GAPS-friendly
DAIRY-FREE
Budget-Friendly

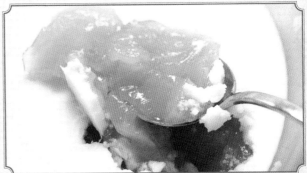

Lamb Stock

3–5 Quarts /2.8–4.7 liters

*L*amb broth is very flavorful and makes any type of soup with lamb especially wonderful. Roasting the vegetables and lamb bones brings even more flavor out in the stock. Lamb bones are best bought straight from farmers, as they generally sell the bones very cheaply or even give them away. I bought several bundles of bones for $2 a pop at my local farmers market recently. My large pot of stock only cost about $3 total! You can also save any lamb bones such as leg of lamb for making stock.

2–3 pounds/.9–1.3 kilograms lamb bones

4 carrots, scrubbed, cut into 2-inch/5-cm pieces

2 celery sticks, cut into 2-inch/5-cm pieces

1 large onion, peeled and quartered

3 garlic cloves, smashed

2 tablespoons fat of your choice (see page 23)

2 bay leaves

1 tablespoon black peppercorns

2–4 tablespoons raw apple cider vinegar, optional

1. Preheat the oven to 400F/205C. In a large oven-safe pot, place the lamb bones, carrots, celery, onion, and garlic. Drizzle the bones with your fat of choice and place the pot in the oven for 30–45 minutes, stirring or turning the bones and vegetables over once, until they start to brown.

2. Take the pot out of the oven and cool until warm. Cover the ingredients with water. Add the bay leaves, peppercorns, and apple cider vinegar (if using).

3. Leave the stock for one hour at room temperature to jump-start the apple cider vinegar action on the bones. (If you are not using vinegar, skip this step.)

4. Place the pot on the stove on high heat and bring it to a boil. Turn the heat to low and cover. Simmer for 3–48 hours and periodically skim any foam or scum from the top.

5. When the stock is done, strain it through a fine sieve or colander into a heat-safe bowl or pot. For a clear broth, use cheesecloth or a coffee filer in the sieve. You can skim fat from the surface of the warm broth with a spoon (or a fat-skimming ladle) or chill the stock and scoop off the congealed fat from the surface.

6. Chill the stock quickly if you are not using right away. Reuse the bones if desired according to the directions on page 42.

GLUTEN-FREE
Grain-free
GAPS-friendly
DAIRY-FREE
Budget-Friendly

Meat Glaze
(Concentrated Stock)

1 cup

Simmering stock for a long time evaporates much of the liquid, resulting in a thick syrup that hardens dramatically once it is chilled. Unlike a stock in full liquid form that lasts only five days in the refrigerator, this concentrate will last three months refrigerated and indefinitely in the freezer. With this on hand, you can add a small spoonful to many types of sauces to give them fuller flavor, or you can add water to reconstitute it into stock to use in soup. No need to have soup bouillon cubes with this on hand! The most important thing is to skim all of the fat thoroughly off the stock and not burn it (which, yes, can happen at the end). For every quart of broth, you will concentrate it down to one-half cup or less. So, you can start with whatever quantity you want, keeping that ratio in mind. For the directions below, I use two quarts and concentrate it to one cup. This method works well with beef, chicken, turkey, and lamb stocks. You can also simply concentrate a stock by half or two-thirds and freeze it. This allows you to freeze stock without it taking up as much room. To use it, simply add water back to the original quantity.

| 2 quarts stock of your choice, chilled |

1. Carefully skim all of the fat off of the surface of the stock with a spoon or skimmer.

2. Strain the stock through cheesecloth to eliminate any pieces of meat or vegetables. (Repeat if needed.) If the stock is very gelatinous, heat it until it has liquefied before straining.

3. Place the de-fatted and skimmed stock in a large pot and place it on the stove, bringing it to a simmer. If any foam appears, skim it off. Simmer the liquid gently until it has reduced by half.

4. Strain it again through the cheesecloth into a medium pot.

5. Simmer it gently until you have about one cup of concentrate and it coats the back of a spoon as a light layer of glaze. Be careful not to burn it.

6. The glaze lasts up to three months refrigerated, indefinitely in the freezer.

Simple Fish Stock

About 3 quarts/2.8 liters

This fish stock takes very little effort. Simply throw everything together in a pot, simmer, and you have a beautiful, light fish stock. I get bones from wild Alaskan halibut or cod from a local store (it costs a couple of dollars per pound), but if you are lucky, you can get them for free. Don't use salmon or other oily fishes when making stock. Sole, flounder, bass, and halibut are some of the traditional types of fish to use for stock.

2–4 pounds/.9–1.8 kilograms fish bones (including heads, if available)

4 celery sticks and leaves, thinly sliced

1–2 yellow onions, quartered

2 carrots, scrubbed, thinly sliced

½ cup/120 ml white wine

1 tablespoon black peppercorns

1½ teaspoons dried thyme or 6–8 sprigs fresh thyme

Handful fresh parsley

2–4 tablespoons raw apple cider vinegar, optional

2 dried bay leaves

1. Place the fish bones and heads, if you have them, in a large stockpot. Add water to the pot until the water reaches 1½ inches above the top of the fish. Bring it to a simmer, but don't boil. Skim any foam from the top.

2. Add the rest of the ingredients and simmer the stock on low heat for 3–12 hours. (While even thirty minutes is sufficient for flavor, you will get more nutrients if you simmer the stock longer.)

3. Strain the stock through a fine sieve into a heat-safe bowl or pot. For a clear broth, use cheesecloth or a coffee filter in the sieve. If needed, skim fat from the surface of the warm broth with a spoon (or a fat-skimming ladle) or chill the stock and scoop off any congealed fat from the surface. Keeps up to three days refrigerated or for several months frozen.

GLUTEN-FREE
Grain-free
GAPS-friendly
DAIRY-FREE
Budget-Friendly

Rich Fish Stock

About 3 quarts/2.8 liters

58 *The sautéed vegetables and steamed fish bones give this broth a richer, fuller flavor, while the Simple Fish Stock is less work and has a lighter flavor. Both are delicious, though this version may be my favorite.*

2 tablespoons/30 grams butter or ghee (or fat of your choice)

2 medium onions, peeled, thinly sliced

2 celery sticks, thinly sliced

2 carrots, scrubbed, thinly sliced

1 tablespoon black peppercorns

1½ teaspoons dried thyme or 6–8 sprigs fresh thyme

Handful parsley

Dash salt

2–4 pounds/.9–1.8 kilograms fish bones, including heads if available, from non-oily fish such as cod or halibut

½ cup/120 ml white wine

2–4 tablespoons raw apple cider vinegar, optional

2 dried bay leaves

1. In a large pot, heat the butter over medium heat until it has melted. Add the onions, celery, carrots, peppercorns, thyme, parsley, and salt and sauté until the vegetables start to soften (5–7 minutes).

2. Add the fish bones and heads, if you have them, on top of the vegetables.

3. Add the wine and cover the pot.

4. Gently steam the fish bones over low or medium-low heat for ten minutes or until the fish bones have turned white.

5. Meanwhile, heat three quarts of water in a separate pot. Once the fish bones and vegetables are steamed, pour it over the fish bones and vegetables until they are just covered. Then, reheat the pot, but don't let it boil. When it just starts to bubble, skim off any foam that has risen to the top and turn the heat to low.

6. Add the vinegar, if using, and bay leaves.

7. Simmer the stock slowly for 3–12 hours. (The longer you cook, the more opportunity you will give the minerals to seep into the stock. For taste, 30 minutes is sufficient, but simmer longer for better nutrition.)

8. When the stock is done, strain it through cheesecloth or a coffee filter in a fine sieve or colander into a heat-safe bowl or pot. If needed, skim fat from the surface of the warm broth with a spoon (or a fat-skimming ladle) or chill the stock and scoop off any congealed fat from the surface.

9. The stock keeps up to three days refrigerated and several months in the freezer.

GLUTEN-FREE
Grain-free
GAPS-friendly
DAIRY-FREE
Budget-Friendly

Anchovy Broth

6 cups/1.4 liters

I was thrilled when I learned about this simple broth. Made out of nutrient-dense and inexpensive dried anchovies, this broth can be made in minutes. Anchovies are quite low in mercury and very nutritious. I often use anchovy broth to make miso soup and other Asian soups instead of the more traditional bonito flakes (made from skipjack tuna, which contains higher amounts of mercury). According to the Marine Conservation Society, most anchovies are considered low-vulnerability, making them a sustainable fish as well.

Dried anchovies aren't found at most supermarkets, however. Your best bet is to visit your local Asian store or buy them online on Amazon.com or www.RadiantLifeCatalog.com. They should have many sizes, so get 2–3-inch anchovies (you can also use dried sardines) for this recipe. This broth is very light in color and smells fairly fishy when being made, so turn on that fan!

10–15 2- to 3-inch/5–7-cm dried sardines or anchovies

1 piece of kombu (dried kelp), optional

7 cups/1.6 liters filtered water

1. Place the dried sardines, kombu (if using), and water in a medium-sized pot. Bring to a boil, turn heat to low, and simmer for 15 minutes.

2. Strain the broth and use it right away or keep it in the refrigerator for up to three days.

Ginger and Garlic Version

Add 3 smashed garlic cloves and a 1- to 2-inch/ 2.5- to 5-cm piece of fresh ginger, thinly sliced with the dried sardines or anchovies.

GLUTEN-FREE
Grain-free
GAPS-friendly
DAIRY-FREE
Budget-Friendly

Light Vegetable Stock

8 cups/1.8 liters

This is a basic and simple vegetable stock that takes just a few minutes to throw together in a pot. When you want a vegetable stock that has a light flavor that won't overwhelm a simple soup, this is the one to use. It is also inexpensive to make. When you want a broth with a deeper flavor, go for either the Roasted Vegetable Broth (page 64) or the Mushroom Broth (page 68).

1 large or 2 small/medium onions, peeled and chopped (sweet onions are a good choice)

4 medium-large carrots, scrubbed, cut into 1-inch/2.5-cm pieces

2 celery sticks and leaves, cut into 1-inch/2.5-cm pieces

3 medium garlic cloves, peeled

2 bay leaves

Handful parsley leaves

2 teaspoons black peppercorns

9 cups/1.9 liters water

1. Place all of the ingredients in a medium-sized pot on medium heat and bring the stock to a simmer.

2. Turn the heat to low, cover the pot, and simmer for 40–60 minutes.

3. Strain the stock through a fine sieve into a heat-safe bowl or pot. It will keep up to five days in the refrigerator.

Vegetarian-
Friendly
GLUTEN-FREE
Grain-free
GAPS-friendly
DAIRY-FREE
Budget-Friendly

Roasted Vegetable Broth

About 6 cups/1.4 liters

Vegetable broths can be as simple as adding some vegetable scraps, a sprinkle of black peppercorns, a sprig of thyme, and a bay leaf into a pot with water and simmering. But if you really want a broth with a deep flavor, roasted vegetables will add a depth that is often missing in vegetable broths. I enjoy this broth so much that I drink it gently warmed and salted all by itself. The mushrooms add an earthiness; the carrots and parsnips add sweetness; and the celery, garlic, and onions add a lot of additional flavor. There is room to play around with the ingredients in this broth, too. It wouldn't be a bad idea to double this recipe either. For a double batch, I recommend that you roast the vegetables in pans so that more vegetables brown. Then, scrape them into the pot when they're done.

4 medium carrots, scrubbed, cut into 2-inch/5-cm pieces

2 medium yellow onions, peeled and quartered

2 celery sticks, cut into 2-inch/5-cm pieces

4 garlic cloves, peeled

1 small-medium parsnip, scrubbed and quartered

8 medium mushrooms (button mushrooms are fine), cut in half

2 tablespoons fat of your choice (see page 23)

Unrefined salt (see page 22)

Freshly ground pepper

1½ teaspoons dried thyme or 6–8 sprigs fresh thyme

Handful fresh parsley

2 bay leaves

1 tablespoon black peppercorns

1. Preheat the oven to 425F/218C. Toss the vegetables in a large ovenproof pot with the fat of your choice. Salt and pepper the vegetables generously.

2. Place the pot uncovered in the middle of the oven. Roast for 40–60 minutes, stirring every 20 minutes or so. When the vegetables start to brown on the edges, remove the pot from the oven and place it on the stovetop.

3. Add enough hot water to the pot to cover the vegetables (about 6–8 cups/1.4–1.8 liters). Add the thyme, parsley, bay leaves, and peppercorns.

4. Bring the broth to a boil and reduce heat to low. Simmer for 30–60 minutes.

5. Strain the broth through a fine sieve over a heat-safe bowl or pot. It keeps up to five days refrigerated.

Vegetarian-
Friendly
GLUTEN-FREE
Grain-free
GAPS-friendly
DAIRY-FREE
Budget-Friendly

Herbed Garlic Broth

8–10 cups/1.9–2.4 liters

This light broth is heavy in flavor and only takes 30 minutes to make. Vary the herbs according to what you have on hand, or think ahead to what type of soup you want to make using the broth. You can also serve the broth simply with a bit of pasta and meatballs, or try ladling it over toast and a poached egg with a topping of Parmesan cheese. It's a great broth when you have a cold and need something soothing.

2 heads of garlic (not cloves)

Handful fresh herbs (a handful of fresh oregano with five sage leaves or thyme is a good choice)

10 cups/2.4 liters water

1. Peel off the outer layers of the garlic. Cut off the top of each garlic bulb to reveal all of the garlic inside.

2. Place them in a medium-sized pot with the fresh herbs and water.

3. Bring the broth to a boil, turn heat to low, and simmer for 30 minutes.

4. Strain the broth and salt it well before serving. It will keep for a week in the refrigerator.

Quick Recipe
Vegetarian-
Friendly
GLUTEN-FREE
Grain-free
GAPS-friendly
DAIRY-FREE
Budget-Friendly

Mushroom Vegetable Broth

14–16 cups/3.3–3.7 liters

Both the dried and fresh mushrooms in this simple vegetable stock give it an earthy and deep flavor with a lot of umami. It is quite delicious and makes a large pot. To make this broth more frugal, save mushroom stems from different kitchen projects and use them in this recipe.

2 medium yellow or sweet onions, peeled and chopped

4 carrots, scrubbed, cut into 1-inch/2.5-cm pieces

4 celery sticks, peeled, cut into 1-inch/2.5-cm pieces

3 garlic cloves, peeled

2 cups quartered mushrooms or mushroom stems

1 tablespoon black or white peppercorns

2 bay leaves

16 cups/3.7 liters filtered water

½ ounce/26 grams dried mushrooms (your choice of variety)

1. Place all of the ingredients in a large pot and bring the broth to a boil on high heat.

2. Turn the heat to low, cover the pot, and simmer for 60 minutes.

3. Strain broth through a fine sieve over a heat-safe bowl or pot. It will keep for one week in the refrigerator.

Vegetarian-
Friendly
GLUTEN-FREE
Grain-free
GAPS-friendly
DAIRY-FREE

Stinging Nettle Broth

Yield Varies

Stinging nettles are full of vitamins and minerals and have been historically used to help the body cleanse in the spring. You can certainly forage for them yourself, which makes this broth practically free! Just make sure you know exactly what you're looking for and the proper foraging procedure. I've also seen bags of nettles for sale in certain stores and farmers markets in the spring. The soy sauce and nutritional yeast bring umami and balance out the flavor nicely. Nutritional yeast is also very nutritious and is especially full of many B vitamins. This recipe provides you with a very restorative broth.

Nettles (amount of choice)

Filtered Water

TO SERVE

Soy sauce or tamari (use tamari for gluten-free option)

Nutritional yeast

1. Using gloves, place the nettles in an appropriately sized pot for the amount of nettles you are using. Cover them with water and bring the broth to a boil on high heat.

2. Turn the heat to low and simmer the broth gently for 1 hour or up to 12 hours. You can also use a slow cooker overnight.

3. When the broth is done, strain the nettles from the broth. You can also gently squeeze the nettles to remove all of the broth from the leaves. Once cooked, they can't sting you.

4. To serve the broth, add 1½–2 teaspoons of soy sauce or tamari and 1 teaspoon of nutritional yeast to every cup of broth.

Simple Thai Broth

6 servings

72

This is a perfect broth when you're coming down with a cold. It has chicken stock, known for its healing properties, and it has coconut milk, which contains MCFAs that have powerful antimicrobial properties. Plus, it contains ginger, garlic, and other spices that ramp up the immune system. You can keep this broth simple with just some ginger and garlic in coconut chicken stock, or you can add more flavor with a stalk of lemongrass (which also gives extra health benefits) or a prepared Thai red curry, which is easy to keep on hand. To make this broth a full meal, serve it over rice pasta and cooked chicken and perhaps some spinach cooked in the broth at the end. This is pretty rich, so cut the coconut milk in half for a lighter broth if desired.

6 cups/1.4 liters chicken stock

1 (14-ounce/414 ml) can full-fat coconut milk

4-inch/10-cm piece of ginger, cut into thin slices, or 2 tablespoons grated ginger

3 garlic cloves, smashed

Pinch or two red chili flakes

FOR MORE FLAVOR

1 stalk lemongrass cut in half

2 teaspoons Thai red curry

TO SERVE

Unrefined salt (page 22) or fish sauce

Fresh limes (optional)

Cilantro (optional)

Sliced green onions (optional)

1. Place the stock, coconut milk, ginger, garlic, and red chili flakes (plus lemongrass and/or Thai red curry, if using) in a large pot on high heat and bring to a boil.

2. Turn down the heat and simmer the broth for ten minutes.

3. Salt the broth with unrefined salt or fish sauce to taste. Remove the lemongrass, ginger (if you used sliced ginger), and garlic. Serve with a slice of lime, chopped cilantro, and/or sliced green onions, if desired.

Quick Recipe
GLUTEN-FREE
Grain-free
DAIRY-FREE
Budget-Friendly

Korean Oxtail Soup

10–12 servings

I enjoy this soup for so many reasons. First, it's delicious in a very simple way. Oxtail is simmered with garlic and fresh ginger, making a rich broth that can be enjoyed with the oxtail meat and a side of rice. I also like that it makes a large pot of broth, considering that oxtail (becoming popular) is getting more expensive. I first made this after my last baby was born, and we enjoyed it for many breakfasts. It's a soothing, nutritious start to the day.

Traditionally, this soup is carefully skimmed of all fat and boiled for a long time to achieve a milky white stock. I simplify it by skipping that last step, as I enjoy the little pools of soft fat in the soup. Because the oxtails aren't browned at all beforehand, this broth has a lighter flavor that is unique. While it's traditional to serve white rice on the side, I also enjoy adding cooked brown or white rice into the broth itself. Just add it with a light hand, as you want it to stay very "brothy."

2½ pounds/1.15 kilograms oxtail (ask your butcher to cut it into 2-inch/5-cm pieces)

2 teaspoons salt

2-inch/5-cm piece of ginger, thinly sliced

6 medium garlic cloves

4 green onions, thinly sliced (green parts only)

Unrefined Salt (page 22)

1. Place the oxtail in a large pot and cover it with cool water. Let it sit for one hour to drain the blood from the oxtail. Drain and rinse the pot.

2. Cover the oxtail again with cold water and place it on high heat, bringing it to a boil.

3. Drain the oxtail and rinse with cool water and rinse the pot out as well to remove any scum. Add 16 cups/3.7 liters of water, the salt, ginger, and garlic to the pot. Bring it to a boil, lower the heat, and simmer gently for at least three hours, or up to 12 hours. This is a great soup to leave on the stove or in a slow cooker all day at this point.

4. When the soup is done, remove the oxtail, ginger, and garlic from the pot. Once the oxtail is cool enough to handle, shred all of the meat, removing the bones and any fat. Add the meat back to the soup and salt to taste. Skim all or some of the fat from the surface of the soup (or chill and remove congealed fat), if desired.

5. Serve the soup topped with the green onions and with rice on the side.

Traditional Method

Traditional method of making the broth milky: Add one or two marrow or knuckle bones with the oxtail to provide more "bone" to the broth, and increase the liquid a bit. Remove the oxtail once the meat is fork-tender and remove all of the meat from the bones, setting the meat aside in the refrigerator. Skim the stock of all fat (for easy removal, chill the broth and remove the congealed fat on the surface). Then, add the oxtail bones back in the pot with the broth and bring to a low, rumbling boil. Boil for 3–12 more hours or until the broth has a whitish tint.

Simple Miso Soup

4 servings as side dishes

We try to make most of our food at home, but when we do eat out, we love to eat sushi. I'm always sure to order a side of miso soup, too. It's light and delicious. We now make family-style sushi at home, and I make a pot of Simple Miso Soup to go with it. We also enjoy Miso Soup as part of our breakfast, a traditional Japanese habit.

You can use whatever type of miso paste you like in this soup. You can also use two different types for a different flavor profile. The white and red miso pastes are two that I currently use. The red is more robust, while the white has a gentler flavor. Make sure you buy naturally fermented organic soybean paste. You can find it at pretty much any health food store. I have also been able to find organic miso paste at my local Asian market. I look for live-culture or raw miso paste. I like anchovy stock the best in this recipe, but I do sometimes use chicken stock. You will have to add significantly more soy sauce or tamari when using chicken stock, as it doesn't contain the natural saltiness of the anchovy stock.

4 cups/.9 liters anchovy stock

2 tablespoons miso paste

2 teaspoons (roughly) wakame (a seaweed that almost instantly expands in hot liquid)

2 tablespoons sliced green onions

¼ cup/68 grams cubed firm tofu

Soy sauce or tamari (use tamari for gluten-free option)

1. In a small pot, heat the anchovy stock on medium heat until hot.

2. Mix about ¼ cup/60 grams of the broth with the miso paste in a small cup until smooth. Stir this mixture into the soup.

3. Add the wakame, green onions, and tofu and heat the soup through. Taste-test and add the soy sauce/tamari, if needed, to add more flavor and saltiness.

The problem with soy

I recommend that you buy all organic soy products because much of soy is now genetically modified. However, I don't recommend that you eat high amounts of soy, as soy is high in antinutrients and controversial phytoestrogens. When you do consume it, eat it in its traditional fermented form such as naturally fermented soy sauce or tamari, miso, etc. Tofu, while fermented, isn't fermented long enough to reduce many of the antinutrients. So, we often leave it out of this recipe. It's such a small amount, however, that I don't feel bad about using it once in a while.

Simple Soups with Eggs

*C*ooks add eggs to simple broths in many different countries. Since eggs are a wonderful and inexpensive source of protein, it's understandable that the practice is so widespread. When you buy eggs from pastured chickens, the yolk will be a deep orange, demonstrating its superior nutritional value. Find them at some high-end or health food stores, farmers markets, or directly from small farms in your area.

The following soups are simple, so I recommend using an especially flavorful broth.

Other soups using eggs:

VEGETARIAN UDON SOUP WITH MUSHROOMS AND EGGS, PAGE 126

CHINESE CONGEE, PAGE 240

Chinese Egg Drop Soup

4–6 small servings

I have always loved the simplicity of this soup in Chinese restaurants. It's the perfect start to a Chinese dinner, especially if the soup and the main dish are homemade! Ginger and garlic are infused into the broth, adding a subtle backdrop. The longer you simmer it, the more pronounced the flavor will become. While Egg Drop Soup tends to be thickened a lot in restaurants, I have only lightly thickened it here for a more subtle approach. You can certainly thicken the soup to your liking or leave out the thickener entirely for a thin version.

4 cups/.9 liters chicken stock

1-inch/2.5-cm fresh ginger, cut into 4 thin slices

3 green onions, sliced (plus more for garnishing, if desired)

3 garlic cloves, peeled and crushed

1 tablespoon organic cornstarch, arrowroot powder, or tapioca starch

1 tablespoon water

1 tablespoon soy sauce or tamari (use tamari for gluten-free option)

Unrefined salt to taste (about ½ teaspoon if using unsalted stock)

White pepper to taste (black pepper can be substituted)

3 large eggs, whisked

1. In a small pot on high heat, bring the chicken stock to a boil and add the ginger, green onions, and garlic to the soup. If desired, you can place the garlic and ginger in a linen bag (generally used for tea) or tie them in cheesecloth for easier removal. Simmer on low, covered, for 5–20 minutes.

2. Remove the garlic and ginger. If they are free-floating, you can use a slotted spoon. Mix the cornstarch, arrowroot powder, or tapioca starch with 1 tablespoon of water. Add the mixture to the soup and whisk. Cook for a couple of minutes to thicken.

3. Add the soy sauce or tamari and salt and pepper to taste.

4. Bring to a simmer and then take the soup off of the heat. Whisk the broth into a small whirlpool, slowly drizzle in the eggs, and leave the soup to set for one minute.

5. Break up the eggs into ribbons with a fork. Taste, and season with salt or pepper if necessary.

Quick Recipe
GLUTEN-FREE
Grain-free
DAIRY-FREE
Budget-Friendly

Stracciatella

4 small servings

I love this simple, traditional soup with Roman roots. I like mine with plenty of pepper, and the nutmeg is optional but adds a warming, subtle flavor. Rather than just eggs making little noodles in the stock, this version has cheese and eggs mixed together, which makes soft, delicious egg-y noodles.

4 cups/.9 liters chicken stock

½–1 teaspoon unrefined salt (leave out if using store-bought broth)

2 large eggs

¼ cup/5 grams freshly grated Parmesan cheese

¼ cup/10 grams chopped parsley

Pinch freshly ground nutmeg (optional)

Freshly ground black or white pepper

1. In a medium pot on low heat, bring the stock and ½ teaspoon salt to a simmer. Taste and adjust the salt if needed. Turn off the heat.

2. Beat the eggs and Parmesan together in a separate small bowl.

3. Whirl the stock around into a small whirlpool with a whisk or wooden spoon and drizzle the egg/Parmesan mixture in the soup slowly, giving it a quick stir when it has all been added.

4. Add the parsley and nutmeg (if using).

5. Let the soup set for 45 seconds in order to cook the egg mixture completely. Gently separate the egg mixture with a fork, if needed, to create finer strands of egg.

6. Taste, and adjust salt as necessary and season with pepper.

Peasant-Style Brussels Sprout and Egg Drop Soup

6 servings

Unlike the first two soups in this section, this one is hearty with the addition of both bread and Brussels sprouts, which add flavor and substance. It's easy to make, and it's the perfect dish after a hard day's work. The fennel seed is a flavorful component, but you can also make it without for a milder version. My recipes testers were split down the middle on whether it was better with or without the fennel seed!

An old-fashioned way to make a soup hardier was to serve it over a piece of day-old bread. I love this practice. Here I use a traditional dark rye made with a long sourdough fermentation process. It was perfect for the soup, though a wide variety of breads would work just as well.

1 pound/450 grams Brussels sprouts

2 tablespoons fat of choice (see page 23)

2 medium/4 small leeks, washed, trimmed, thinly sliced (see page 33)

Unrefined salt

5 cups/1.15 liters chicken stock

¾ teaspoon fennel seed (optional)

4 large eggs

Freshly ground pepper

To serve

6 slices of hearty bread, toasted

Parmigiano-Reggiano or Parmesan cheese, freshly shredded (optional)

Finely minced parsley (optional)

1. Cut off the stems of the Brussels sprouts and shred them by hand or with a food processor.

2. In a large pot, add your fat of choice and heat it over medium or medium-high heat until hot but not smoking.

3. Add the shredded Brussels sprouts and leeks, sprinkle them generously with salt, and sauté for 5–7 minutes or until the vegetables are limp. Stir as needed to prevent browning and promote even cooking.

4. Add the chicken stock and fennel seed (if using) and bring the soup to a boil over high heat. Turn the heat to low, cover, and cook for about 5 minutes or until the vegetables are soft.

5. Meanwhile, beat the eggs in a medium-sized bowl.

6. Turn off the heat under the soup and gently drizzle the eggs into the soup while stirring with a fork to break the eggs into small strands as they cook. Let the soup stand for 45 seconds.

7. Salt and pepper to taste.

8. In each soup bowl, place a piece of toasted bread, cover with soup, and sprinkle generously with cheese and parsley (if using).

Greek Lemon Soup

4–6 servings

86

This traditional Greek soup is the perfect trinity of sour, salty, and rich. It has all of the qualities of a good comfort soup. The eggs add creaminess and richness, and the lemon brightens it up. Sometimes I'm in the mood for an especially tart soup, so I add significantly more lemon juice (as much as ¼ cup extra). The most important thing is to adjust the flavors at the end so that the sour points of the soup are balanced out by the saltiness. You can make this soup quite thick with rice, but I love the broth so much that I generally keep the rice to a minimum. This soup is different because instead of making the eggs into threads, you temper the eggs to enhance the soup with their rich flavor without curdling them. This soup works well without the rice, for a grain-free and GAPS-friendly version as well.

8 cups/1.9 liters chicken stock

1½–2 teaspoons unrefined salt (skip if using store-bought broth)

¼ cup/45 grams long-grain white rice*

¼ cup/60 ml to ½ cup/120 ml fresh lemon juice (about three lemons for ½ cup/120 ml)

3 large eggs

3 tablespoons or more finely minced parsley

1. In a medium/large pot, heat the chicken stock and salt over high heat, until simmering.

2. Add the rice and simmer on low, covered, for 20 minutes.

3. Add ¼ cup/60 ml of lemon juice.

4. In a large, heat-safe bowl, whisk the 3 eggs until smooth.

5. In a slow drizzle, add 1 cup/236 ml of the soup to the bowl, while whisking at the same time. This tempers the egg mixture.

6. Drizzle 3 more cups of the stock into the bowl, again whisking at the same time.

7. Return the soup to the pot, continuing to whisk it to prevent the eggs from curdling. If needed, you can gently reheat the soup, but it should still be plenty hot. If the eggs start to separate, take the pot off of the heat and whisk like mad. If you accidently curdle the eggs, not to worry, this soup is still delicious.

8. Add the parsley and adjust the flavors with lemon juice and salt as needed.

*If you'd like to use brown rice, I recommend using precooked. Add ½–¾ cup /105-160 grams of precooked brown rice and simply heat it through instead of the 20 minutes of cook time. You can also use precooked white rice the same way.

Spanish Garlic Soup

4 small servings

Traditionally served to those nursing a hangover or cold, this soup is simple to prepare and full of comforting nourishment. Smoked paprika adds a subtle flavor, and the herbs provide Spanish flair to an otherwise basic but delicious soup. Smoked paprika can sometimes be found in the bulk herb and spice section of health food and specialty stores, which allows you to buy just a small amount if you don't use it often. Red pepper flakes make a good substitute.

2 tablespoons olive oil or other fat of choice (see page 23)

3–6 medium garlic cloves (3 for a mild flavor, 6 for garlic lovers)

1 tablespoon finely minced fresh rosemary or ½ tablespoon finely minced dried rosemary

¾–1 teaspoon unrefined salt (omit if using store-bought stock)

4 cups/.9 liters chicken stock (or vegetarian broth of choice—you could use Herbed Garlic Broth on page 66 if you love garlic especially)

½ teaspoon smoked paprika or a generous pinch of dried red pepper flakes

½ teaspoon dried oregano

4 large eggs

TO SERVE

4 pieces of bread, toasted (a crusty, rustic bread works well)

1. In a medium-sized pot, heat the oil until hot. Add the garlic, rosemary, and a pinch of salt. Sauté for 1–2 minutes or until the garlic just begins to turn brown.

2. Add the stock right away, followed by the paprika, oregano, and remaining salt. Bring to a low simmer over medium-high heat, turn the heat to low, and simmer for 10 minutes. Taste and add more salt if needed and keep the soup warm as you cook the eggs.

3. Fill a medium saucepan ¾ full of water. Bring it to a simmer over medium-high heat. Crack the eggs into the simmering water and return it to a simmer for 4 minutes (for slightly runny yolks).

4. Meanwhile, place a piece of bread at the bottom of four bowls, cutting the bread in half to fit, if needed.

5. When the eggs are done, remove them with a slotted spoon and place one in each bowl. Divide the hot broth into the four bowls and serve.

Vegetarian-
Friendly
Quick Recipe
DAIRY-FREE
Budget-Friendly

Family Favorite Soups and Stews

It was difficult to choose which soups to put in this section because we have so many favorites. In the end, I decided to include the recipes that I have used for many years or that have been handed down in either my family or in my husband's family. These recipes have stood the test of time. While we have added plenty of new favorite soups and stews in the last couple of years, these remain on our menu on a regular basis. You will find the majority of them to be quite simple to make, which is yet another reason why they appear on our table over and over. I hope you and yours enjoy them as much as we do.

A few other family favorites:

PHO GA (CHICKEN NOODLE SOUP), PAGE 130

SIMPLE CREAM OF TOMATO SOUP, PAGE 142

EGYPTIAN RED LENTIL SOUP WITH CARAMELIZED ONIONS, PAGE 160

LEEK AND POTATO SOUP, PAGE 208

CHINESE CONGEE, PAGE 240

Italian Zucchini and Sausage Soup

6 servings

This simple soup comes from my mother-in-law and sister-in-law. It's a great family favorite that's both simple and hearty, especially when served with buttered bread and a green salad. It is one of those soups that we would be happy to eat every week.

1 pound/450 grams mild bulk Italian sausage (pork, turkey, or chicken; remove from casings, if necessary)

4 cups/.9 liters chicken or beef stock

3 medium garlic cloves, peeled and finely minced

4–6 sticks celery, trimmed and thinly sliced

5 medium zucchini squash, halved and thinly sliced

1 onion, peeled and chopped

2 cups/475 ml diced tomatoes, canned or fresh

1 teaspoon Italian seasoning

1 teaspoon dried oregano

½ teaspoon dried basil

1 teaspoon unrefined salt (less if using store-bought stock)

Ground pepper

1. Brown the sausage in a large pot over medium heat. If you're using turkey or chicken sausage, you will probably need to use a little bit of fat or oil to prevent it from sticking.

2. Add all of the rest of the ingredients to the cooked sausage and bring the soup to a boil over high heat.

3. Turn the heat to low and simmer, covered, for 20–30 minutes or until the vegetables are soft.

4. Salt and pepper to taste and serve. This soup, like most, is even better after a night in the refrigerator.

Chicken Noodle Soup— Three Ways

94

Chicken noodle soup is one of those classic meals to eat when you feel under the weather. Not only is it soothing, but the nutritious, homemade broth also gives a boost to your immune system. All three of these recipes for chicken noodle soup are simple. One uses premade chicken stock, while another makes a broth while you cook the soup, and the other uses vegetable noodles. I generally garnish it with parsley, but fresh basil is amazing as well.

No Premade Broth Version

8–10 servings

2 tablespoons fat of your choice (see page 23)

1 medium yellow onion, peeled and chopped

4 carrots, peeled and cut into 1-inch/2.5-cm pieces

4 celery sticks, cut into 1-inch/2.5-cm pieces

3 garlic cloves, peeled and finely minced (by hand or in garlic press)

1½–2 pounds/450–680 grams chicken drumsticks

3 quarts/2.8 liters filtered water

1 teaspoon dried (not ground) thyme

2 bay leaves

2 teaspoons unrefined salt

4 ounces/113 grams dried pasta of your choice (we like brown rice spiral noodles) or 1 recipe Sprouted Egg Noodles (see page 36)

Ground pepper

Parsley or basil for garnish

1. In a large pot, heat the fat of your choice over medium to medium-high heat until hot.

2. Add the onion, carrots, celery, and garlic and sprinkle them lightly with salt. Sauté for 5–7 minutes or until soft, stirring as needed to prevent burning.

3. Add the remaining ingredients, except for the pasta and herb garnish, and bring the soup to a boil. Turn the heat to low and simmer gently, covered, for 1 to 1½ hours.

4. Remove the chicken drumsticks and set aside to cool. When they are cool enough to handle, remove the skin, shred the chicken into bite-sized pieces, and add the chicken meat back into the pot. Save the bones for making into stock.

5. Meanwhile, cook the pasta by adding it right into the pot. For dried pasta, cook according to the package directions. If using Sprouted Egg Noodles (page 36), cook for about 5 minutes or until the noodles are tender.

6. Salt and pepper to taste. Garnish with the herb of choice and serve.

DAIRY-FREE
Budget-Friendly

Vegetable Noodle Soup

4 large servings

2 tablespoons fat of your choice (see page 23)

1 medium yellow onion, peeled and chopped

2 celery sticks, thinly sliced

2 garlic cloves, peeled and finely minced by hand or in garlic press

¾ teaspoon dried (not ground) thyme

6 cups/1.4 liters chicken stock

1½ cups/210 grams leftover shredded chicken or 1½ cups/280 grams cubed raw chicken breasts or thighs

4 cups total (4 large handfuls) carrot and/or zucchini noodles (see page 35)

1 teaspoon unrefined salt

Ground pepper

Parsley or basil for garnish

1. In a medium or large pot, heat the fat of your choice over medium to medium-high heat until hot.

2. Add the onion, celery, and garlic and sprinkle them with salt. Sauté for 5–7 minutes or until the vegetables are soft, stirring as needed to prevent burning or browning.

3. Add the dried thyme and chicken stock to the pot. Bring the soup to a boil, turn the heat to low, and simmer for 10 minutes.

4. If you're using raw chicken, add it to the soup and simmer for another 5 minutes or until the chicken is cooked through.

5. If you're using carrot noodles, add them next and cook for 3 minutes.

6. Add the zucchini noodles and cooked chicken (if using) and cook for 3 more minutes or until heated through.

7. Salt and pepper to taste. Garnish the soup with the herb of your choice and serve.

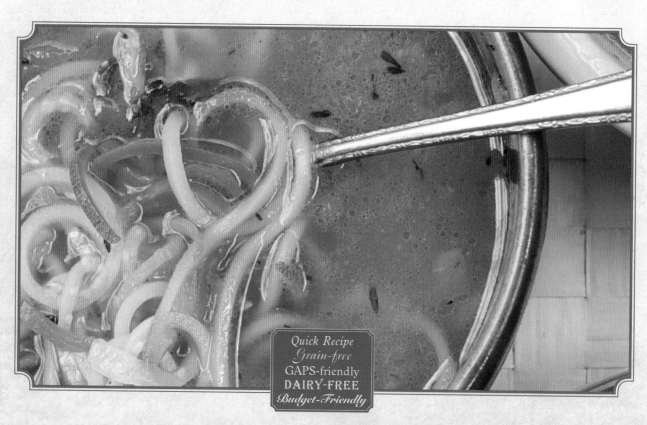

Quick Recipe
Grain-free
GAPS-friendly
DAIRY-FREE
Budget-Friendly

Simple Chicken Noodle Soup

4-6 servings

2 tablespoons fat of your choice (see page 23)

1 medium yellow onion, peeled and chopped

4 carrots, peeled and diced

2 celery sticks, thinly sliced or diced

3 garlic cloves, peeled and finely minced by hand or in garlic press

1 teaspoon dried (not ground) thyme

2 bay leaves

8 cups/1.9 liters chicken stock

2 cups/280 grams chicken, cooked and shredded or 2 cups/370 grams cubed raw chicken breasts or thighs

Half Sprouted Egg Noodle recipe (see page 36) or 3 ounces/85 grams dried pasta

Chopped fresh basil or parsley for garnish

1. In a large pot, heat the fat of your choice over medium to medium-high heat until hot.

2. Add the onion, carrots, celery, and garlic and sprinkle lightly with salt. Sauté for 5–7 minutes or until soft, stirring as needed to prevent burning.

3. Add the thyme, bay leaves, and chicken stock and bring it to a boil. Turn the heat to low and simmer, covered, for 10 minutes or until the vegetables are fork-tender.

4. If you're using raw chicken, add it now and cook for about 5 minutes or until the chicken is cooked all the way through. If you're using precooked chicken, add it and heat through.

5. If you're using fresh pasta, cook it right in the pot for 5 minutes or until the pasta is tender. If you're using dried pasta, cook it in a separate pot according to the package directions, strain it, and add the cooked noodles to the soup.

6. Salt and pepper to taste, garnish the soup with the herb of your choice, and serve.

Grain-free
DAIRY-FREE
Budget-Friendly

Mexican Tortilla Soup

10–12 servings

A version of this recipe has been in our family for the last twenty-five years. It has long been enjoyed and can easily be adapted to your preferences. The garnishes are fun to vary, too. For a thin soup, use ¼ cup/45 grams of brown rice. For a thick version, use ¾ cup/160 grams. Keep in mind that the rice will continue to absorb moisture, so the soup will become thicker and thicker the longer it sits. This makes a large pot, so we often prepare it when having guests over for lunch or dinner.

¼–¾ cup/45–140 grams long-grain brown rice or white rice

1 cup/236 ml warm filtered water

1 tablespoon raw apple cider vinegar, yogurt, kefir, buttermilk, or other live-cultured product

2 tablespoons fat of your choice (see page 23)

1 large yellow onion, peeled and chopped

1 red bell pepper, stemmed, seeded, and chopped

3 garlic cloves, peeled and finely minced by hand or in a garlic press

10 cups/2.4 liters chicken stock or a combination of stock and filtered water

3 cups/710 ml chopped tomatoes, fresh or canned (I use Pomi's chopped tomatoes, 26-ounce size)

2 teaspoons ground cumin

2 teaspoons dried oregano

2 teaspoons salt

¼–¾ teaspoon cayenne pepper (For extra mild, try ⅛ teaspoon; add more if you prefer it spicy)

2 cups/280 grams chicken, cooked and shredded or 2 cups/370 grams cubed raw chicken breasts or thighs

1 cup/226 grams corn, frozen or cut off the cob

YOUR CHOICE OF GARNISHES

Cubed avocado

Chopped cilantro

Shredded cheddar cheese or crumbled queso fresco

Lime wedges

Sour cream

Tortilla chips

1. Combine the rice, warm filtered water, and live cultured product in a nonreactive bowl and cover. Leave it in a warm place for 12–24 hours.

2. After the time has passed, rinse the rice well in a fine sieve. (If you're using white rice, you can skip the soaking step.)

3. In a large pot, heat the fat of your choice over medium to medium-high heat until hot.

4. Add the onion, red bell pepper, and garlic. Sprinkle with salt and sauté, stirring as needed to prevent burning, until the vegetables are soft.

5. Add the remaining ingredients except for the chicken and corn. Bring the soup to a boil, lower the heat, cover, and simmer the soup for 45 minutes or until the rice is cooked (20 minutes if using white rice).

6. Add the chicken and corn and cook for a few more minutes to heat through. If you're using raw chicken, cook the soup until the chicken is cooked through (at least five minutes).

7. Salt generously to taste and serve with the garnishes of your choice.

GLUTEN-FREE
DAIRY-FREE
Budget-Friendly

⌒∽ *Precooked rice variation* ∽⌒

If you have leftover rice to use in this soup, you can finish it in a jiffy, and the rice won't soak up too much of the stock. For Step 2, just simmer for about 15 minutes (solely to give the flavors a bit of time to meld together) and leave the rice out. When you serve, put a generous spoonful or two of cooked rice (it can be cold because the soup will heat it) on the bottom of each person's bowl and ladle the soup over it. This will also stretch the soup out even more to serve more people since the broth won't be absorbed into the rice before serving.

Cream of Vegetable Soup

6–8 servings

This gentle soup has long been a favorite of my daughter, Elena. Now, Aria, who is not quite two, has begun to appreciate this recipe as well. Finish it with a bit of cream or let people drizzle the cream or, better yet, crème fraîche into their own bowls. Not only does the cream add some flair and flavor, but that healthy fat helps you (and/or your children) absorb all of the fat-soluble nutrients in the soup. For a dairy-free version, add a chopped and peeled potato or two, which makes the soup creamier in texture, or try it with about ½ cup/120 ml of almond milk (see page 292).

2 tablespoons fat of your choice (see page 23)

1 medium yellow onion, peeled and chopped

3 garlic cloves, peeled and finely minced by hand or in a garlic press

6 small/medium carrots, peeled and diced

4 large celery sticks, thinly sliced or diced

6 cups/1.4 liters chicken, beef, or vegetarian stock

1 teaspoon dried (not ground) thyme or several sprigs of fresh thyme

2 bay leaves

4 small/medium zucchini squash, diced into small pieces

¼–⅓ cup/60–80 ml cream or crème fraîche for garnish (see page 282) (optional)

1. In a large or medium-sized pot, heat the fat of your choice over medium to medium-high heat until hot. Add the onion, garlic, carrots, and celery. Sprinkle with salt and sauté, stirring as needed to prevent burning, until the vegetables are quite soft (about 7 minutes).

2. Add the stock, thyme, bay leaves, and zucchini and bring the soup to a boil. Turn the heat to low and simmer, covered, for 10 minutes or until the vegetables are tender. Remove the bay leaves.

3. Purée the soup in batches in a blender or food processor. Be careful, as the hot liquid tends to splatter. You can also use an immersion blender to purée the soup in the pot if you prefer. Purée until the soup is very smooth.

4. Salt and pepper to taste.

5. Add the cream (if using) and serve.

Quick Recipe
Vegetarian-
Friendly
GLUTEN-FREE
Grain-free
GAPS-friendly
DAIRY-FREE
Budget-Friendly

Family Favorite Beef Stew

6 servings or up to 10 servings when served over rice or mashed potatoes

This delicious stew is very simple to make. It also only uses one pound of beef for the whole pot (many recipes use 3–5 pounds of beef to serve the same amount of people). I cut my stew meat into smaller pieces at ½-inch/1.25-cm because I prefer the texture. Plus, it makes the beef "stretch" more easily. The first few vegetables that are finely diced are put in for flavor, while the rest are more to bulk up the stew.

1 pound/450 grams beef stew meat, cut into small pieces (½-inch/1.25-cm)

⅓ cup/30 grams unbleached white flour, rice flour, sprouted flour, or arrowroot powder

2 tablespoons fat of your choice (see page 23)

1 large celery stick, diced small

1 large carrot, diced small

1 yellow onion, finely chopped

3 garlic cloves, finely minced by hand or crushed in a garlic press

1 teaspoon dried (not ground) thyme

1 teaspoon dried oregano

3 cups/710 ml canned or fresh chopped tomatoes

2 cups/470 ml dry red wine

2 cups/470 ml beef or chicken stock or a combination of stock and water

2 bay leaves

1½ teaspoons unrefined salt (leave out if using store-bought stock)

4 carrots, peeled, sliced into 1-inch/2.5-cm pieces on a diagonal

4 potatoes, diced into 1-inch/2.5-cm cubes

4 celery sticks, sliced into 1-inch/2.5-cm pieces on a diagonal

1 cup/226 grams corn, fresh or frozen

¼ cup/10 grams minced parsley (optional)

1. Rinse the stew meat and pat it dry with paper towels.

2. In a pie pan or other shallow dish, add the flour and season it with salt and pepper (a generous sprinkle of both will do). Toss the stew meat with the flour mixture.

3. In a large soup pot, heat the fat of your choice until hot over medium to medium-high heat and add the finely diced celery and carrot, plus the onion, and garlic. Sprinkle with salt and sauté for 5 minutes, stirring to prevent burning.

4. When done, remove the vegetables from the pan.

5. Add more fat, if needed, to coat the bottom of the pan. Add the meat and brown on all sides, stirring every minute or so.

6. Add the thyme, oregano, tomatoes, wine, stock, bay leaves, salt, and sautéed vegetables. Bring the soup to a simmer, scraping any browned bits off of the bottom as it heats. Turn the heat to low and simmer, covered, for 45 minutes.

7. Add the rest of the carrots, potatoes, and celery and cook for 30 minutes or until the vegetables and meat are fork tender.

8. Next, add the corn and cook for a few minutes more.

9. Salt and pepper to taste and garnish with the parsley (if using).

10. Serve over rice (see pages 295–297) or mashed potatoes (see page 290)

GLUTEN-FREE
DAIRY-FREE
Budget-Friendly

❦ *Variations* ❧

Extra Meaty: If you want to bulk the stew up with more meat, use up to 2 pounds more and cut down on some of the vegetables.

Spicy: For a little extra spice, add a generous sprinkle of red pepper flakes in Step 2.

Tomato-Free: If you are sensitive to tomatoes, add a bit more wine and more broth to make up for the cooking liquid difference.

New England Clam Chowder

6–8 servings

I grew up enjoying New England Clam Chowder in all of its bacon-y, creamy glory. I especially like the gentleness of this soup, which makes it a great choice for introducing seafood to children. We've always simply let the butter and cream or whole milk thicken the chowder softly, but if you would like thick chowder, add ⅓ cup/30 grams of flour to the sautéed vegetables. Then, stir to coat before adding in the potatoes and stock. This recipe has fresh clams that are added straight to the pot. It makes a very pretty and shell-full chowder. Please serve on a plate large enough for people to place empty clamshells as they enjoy their soup. If you prefer your chowder with more clams, or shell-free, follow the shell-free option below. Refer to page 222 for the proper care of clams, or feel free to use clam juice and canned clams.

6 slices of bacon, diced

4 celery sticks, thinly sliced

1 medium yellow onion, peeled and chopped

12 medium red potatoes, peeled and diced

4 cups/.9 liters Rich Fish Stock (page 58), Simple Fish Stock (page 56), Anchovy Stock (page 60), or Chicken Stock (page 44)

1½ teaspoons dried (not ground) thyme or 6–8 sprigs fresh thyme

2–4 tablespoons of butter or ghee (leave out for dairy free) (optional)

2 cups/470 ml whole milk, half-and-half, or cream (as unprocessed as possible, not ultra-pasteurized) or homemade almond milk (see page 292)

1½–2 pounds/680 to 910 grams fresh, small Manila clams, freshly scrubbed, free of cracks, firmly closed, and free of sand

Minced fresh parsley and/or thyme for garnish (optional)

1. In a large pot, fry the bacon until crispy over medium heat, stirring as needed to cook evenly. Remove the bacon with a slotted spoon and set on a paper towel–lined plate to cool.

2. Leave 2 tablespoons of grease in the pot, removing any extra. Sauté the celery and onion over medium heat in the bacon grease until soft, stirring to prevent burning.

3. Add the potatoes, stock, thyme, crumbled bacon, and butter or ghee (if using).

4. Salt and pepper to taste and bring to a simmer over high heat. Turn the heat to low and simmer for about 15 minutes or until the potatoes are soft.

5. Add the milk or cream and reheat the soup until hot.

6. Add the clams and cook until the clam shells are wide open. (4–5 minutes for small.) Remove any clams that didn't open.

7. Add more salt and pepper if necessary (freshly ground pepper is delicious in clam chowder), and garnish with minced fresh parsley and/or thyme. The flavors will meld more if chilled overnight.

GLUTEN-FREE
Grain-free
DAIRY-FREE

Shell-free Clam Chowder

There are two advantages to shell-free clam chowder. Some people find the shells to be annoying, and you can fit far more clams in your soup without the shells. Granted, this is much more expensive, but it's also more satisfying. For a shell-free clam chowder, start with 5 pounds/2.25 kilograms of Manila clams. In a large pot, heat 1 cup/236 ml of water until just simmering. Add the clams and simmer until all of the clamshells are open. Remove any that didn't open (about 5 minutes). Strain the clams from the water and save the water for use as part of the stock in the soup. Scoop out the clams when they are cool enough to handle and chop them into smaller pieces or leave whole according to your preference. Add them to the soup at the very end, heating until just heated through (overcooking causes them to be chewy).

Version Using Canned Clams

Instead of the fresh clams, use two 6½-ounce/192 ml cans of minced or small whole clams. Look for all-natural, preservative-free clams in their own juice. Drain and save the juice. Then, add the juice as part of the liquid amount. Add the clams at the end of the cooking time and heat through.

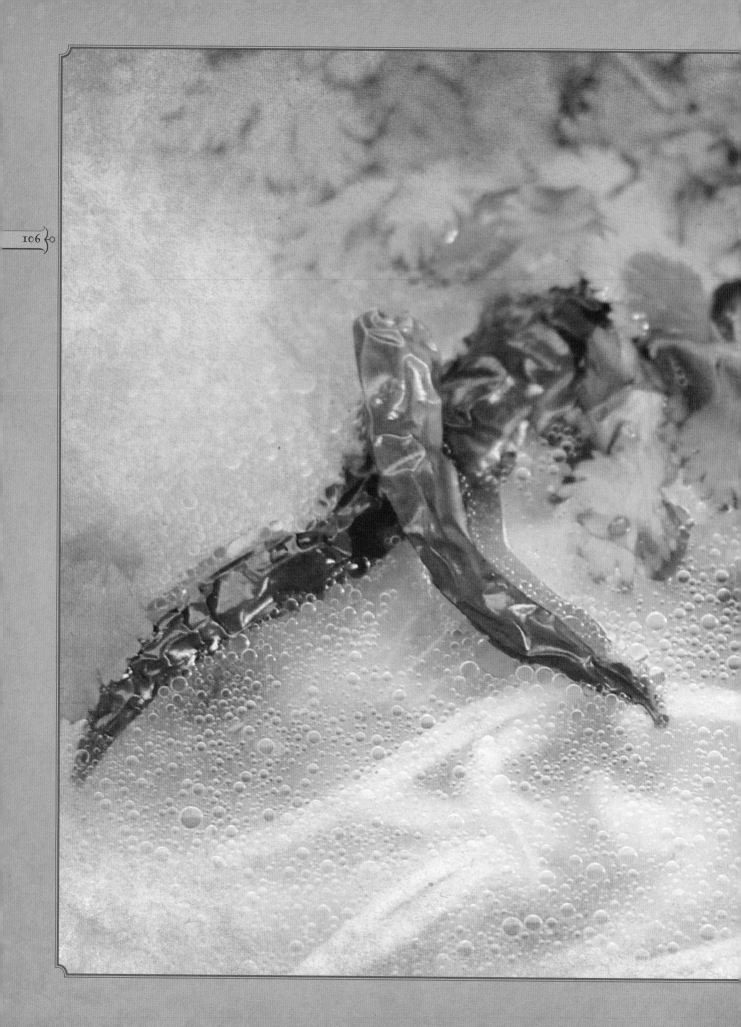

Soups Inspired By Our Favorite Restaurants

It is always so much fun to be introduced to new soups at a restaurant and come home to work at reinventing them. Often, I find that I like my own version even better, which is especially exciting since it can be so much cheaper to make it at home. While I don't enjoy certain restaurant soups, some of my absolute favorite recipes were introduced to me while eating out. The following recipes are from a wide variety of backgrounds, which shows just a little about my family's eating habits.

Other recipes partly inspired by soups I enjoyed at a restaurant:

GREEK LEMON SOUP, PAGE 86

MISO UDON AND CHICKEN SOUP, PAGE 124

LEMONGRASS CLAM CHOWDER, PAGE 224

CLAMS IN A SPICY TOMATO BROTH WITH BACON, PAGE 236

German Lentil Soup

8–10 servings

There is a German restaurant near us that has a simple and gently flavored, yet filling, lentil soup. It's a favorite of mine, and this recipe is my version. Lentils are low in phytic acid and quick cooking, so they don't have to be soaked overnight, though it's still my preference. You will need to add more liquid if you didn't presoak them. You can also add a strip of kombu for digestibility and extra nutrition, but it's completely optional. Kombu was surely not in the original German lentil soup! The nutmeg is what gives it a special flavor.

4 slices thick bacon, nitrate-free

2 small/1 large yellow onion, peeled and chopped

6 medium carrots, peeled and diced or thinly sliced

3 garlic cloves, peeled and finely minced by hand or in a garlic press

6 medium potatoes, peeled or scrubbed and diced (you can also leave the skin on)

2 bay leaves

2 teaspoons cumin

⅛ teaspoon nutmeg, freshly grated preferred

1½ teaspoons dried (not ground) thyme

2 cups/450 grams of green or brown lentils, soaked for 12–24 hours in warm water in a warm place, drained and rinsed (soaking optional)

6 cups/1.4 liters chicken or beef stock or combination of water and stock (use 8 cups/1.9 liters if you did not soak the lentils)

1. In a large pot over medium heat, cook the bacon until crispy, flipping as needed to cook evenly. Remove the bacon, place on a paper towel–lined plate, and then crumble when cooled.

2. Drain all but 2 tablespoons of the extra bacon grease from the pan.

3. Over medium to medium-high heat, sauté the onions, carrots, and garlic in the bacon grease for about 5 minutes or until softened. Stir as needed to prevent burning.

4. Add the potatoes, bay leaves, cumin, nutmeg, thyme, soaked lentils, crumbled bacon, and broth/water. Bring the soup to a boil, turn the heat to low, and cover. Cook for 45–60 minutes or until the lentils are soft. Add up to 2 cups more water if using unsoaked lentils. Add more water, if needed, if the soup becomes too thick.

5. Salt and pepper to taste and serve.

⚜ Other serving ideas ⚜

I generally love adding a drizzle of balsamic vinegar to lentil soups, but this one is great without it. However, if you'd like a little more tang, feel free to finish the soup with a 1–2 tablespoons of vinegar. You can also sprinkle Parmesan or a similar cheese over each individual bowl or provide the cheese at the table for your guests to sprinkle over their bowls.

GLUTEN-FREE
Grain-free
DAIRY-FREE
Budget-Friendly

Tom Yum Gai
(Thai Hot and Sour Soup with Chicken)

6 servings

This soup is easy to make, full of sour and hot notes, and the perfect start to a Thai feast. To make this recipe correctly, fresh galangal should be used, but ginger is a good substitute. I bought a whole bag of dried Thai peppers at my local Asian store for just a couple of dollars—certainly a worthwhile purchase. You can buy dried chilies from Amazon.com and other online stores as well.

This soup is a balance of hot, sour, salty, and sweet, and it's easily adapted based on your preference. Follow the recipe below for a mild version and serve it with chili flakes and lime juice on the side for those who want it more hot or sour. When polled on Facebook, I found that more people liked their Tom Yum Gai without tomatoes. However, if you like yours with tomatoes, simply add 1 cup/226 grams of grape tomatoes (whole) or 2 medium tomatoes cut into eighths along with the lemongrass and chicken.

4 shallots

10–12 dried Thai chili peppers

2 tablespoons fat of your choice (see page 23)

8 cups/1.9 liters filtered water

¾ pound/340 grams boneless, skinless chicken breasts or chicken thighs

2 lemongrass stalks, cut in half

3-inch/7.5-cm piece fresh galangal or fresh ginger, sliced into ½-inch/1.25-cm pieces

6–8 fresh Kaffir lime leaves (or twice as many dried)

4–5 green onions, trimmed and cut into 2-inch/5-cm pieces

1 baby bok choy, rinsed and cut into ½-inch/1.25-cm pieces

8 ounces/226 grams mushrooms (enoki, shitake, or your choice), trimmed and thinly sliced (If using enoki mushrooms, cut into 1½-inch/3.8-cm pieces)

¼ cup plus 2 tablespoons/90 ml fish sauce*

¼ cup plus 2 tablespoons/90 ml of fresh lime juice

1 tablespoon coconut or palm sugar (or sweetener of your choice)

Cilantro for garnish

Lime wedges

1. In a small cast-iron pan, place the shallots (with the peel) and 6 Thai chili peppers and turn the heat to medium. Turn the peppers and shallots over until the peppers are dark but not burnt.

2. Remove peppers and continue to cook the shallots.

3. When the peppers are cool, crumble or crush them carefully in a mortar and pestle. Try to avoid getting the chili pepper dust in the air, as it will tickle your throat.

4. Keep turning the shallots over until the peel is dark and burnt in places. Remove them to cool. When they are cool enough to handle, peel them and cut them in half.

5. Meanwhile, in a large pot, heat 2 tablespoons of the fat of your choice over medium to medium-high heat. When hot, add 4–6 of the dried chili peppers to the oil. Sauté the peppers until they are browned and the oil has been spiced. Remove and discard the peppers.

6. Add the water, chicken, lemongrass, galangal or ginger, Kaffir lime leaves, green onions,

GLUTEN-FREE
Grain-free
DAIRY-FREE

and peeled shallots to the pot. Bring the soup to a boil and turn the heat to low. Keep the soup at a low simmer.

7. After five minutes, add the bok choy and mushrooms. Cook for another five minutes.

8. Remove the chicken with a slotted spoon and place it on a cutting board.

9. Add the fish sauce, ¼ cup of the lime juice, and sweetener to the pot of soup. Taste, and adjust the flavors with the remaining 2 tablespoons of lime juice, more fish sauce, or more sweetener.

10. Dice the chicken on the cutting board and add it back to the pot.

11. Remove the lemongrass (and Kaffir lime leaves and ginger, if desired) from the soup. Serve it with cilantro and lime wedges, as well as extra crumbled Thai chili peppers on the side.

*Fish Sauce

Some brands contain MSG or other undesirable ingredients. I have used and liked Thai Kitchen's "Premium Fish Sauce" and Roland's Fish Sauce. Some of the cheap brands are too overwhelming in flavor.

French Onion Soup

6 servings

While many of us now associate French Onion Soup with either posh restaurants or an unfortunate diner version, its roots go way back. Onion soup was always popular with the poorer classes because onions were cheap, as well as flavorful. The onion-flavored broth was topped with bread to make it more filling and cheese to make it more nutritious and tasty. What was a poor man's feast in former times makes a lovely first course today for an elegant dinner or a light lunch by itself.

The secret to the soup is making sure that you caramelize the onions well. This takes time, and I always set the timer, just to make sure that I don't rush the process. I haven't found anything better than the original way to serve the soup, as the bread and cheese really make it. However, I found that it's almost as good with just the toast for a dairy-free version, and my gluten- and dairy-free daughter enjoys it with cooked rice added.

I almost like this soup over-salted, which is rare for me. Since it depends on so few ingredients, make sure that you use a good-tasting beef stock (I recommend homemade) and a nice wine. It doesn't have to be expensive, but it should be good enough to drink, not just a cooking wine. This soup is just slightly thickened with the addition of flour, but you can leave that step out if desired.

You can use whatever type of bread you want, whether a sourdough whole wheat bread or the more typical baguette, which I use here. Many restaurants and home recipes call for putting the bowls of soup in the oven to melt the cheese on the toast. I find it simpler to melt the cheese on the toast and transfer the toast to the bowls.

2 tablespoons fat of your choice (see page 23)

5 cups/650 grams peeled, thinly sliced red or sweet onions

2–3 medium cloves garlic, peeled and finely minced by hand or in a garlic press

2 tablespoons unbleached white flour, white rice flour, or sprouted flour of choice

1 cup/236 ml dry red wine

6 cups/1.4 liters beef stock

2 bay leaves

2 sprigs fresh thyme or ¾ teaspoon dried (not ground) thyme

TO SERVE

1 thin baguette, thinly sliced to make about 18 slices (or 6 slices if a large baguette)

¾–1 cup/340–450 grams grated Gruyère, Comte, or Emmental cheese

2 tablespoons finely grated Parmigiano-Reggiano or Parmesan cheese (optional)

1. In a large pot, melt the fat of your choice over medium heat until hot. Add the onions and sprinkle them generously with salt. Set a timer for 20 minutes and stir the onions as needed to prevent sticking or premature browning. You want the onions to turn limp and super-soft and start turning a deep brown color. You can also sprinkle ¼ teaspoon of organic white sugar over the

onions to help them caramelize after about 15 minutes of cooking, but it isn't necessary.

2. When the onions look done (you may need up to 30 minutes), add the garlic and cook for one minute more. Then add the flour and stir to coat the onions well with the flour. Cook for 1–2 minutes.

3. Add the wine and allow it to simmer until evaporated, stirring to release any browned bits off the bottom of the pan as the pot is deglazed.

4. Add the beef stock, bay leaves, and thyme and bring the soup to a simmer. Turn the heat to low and cook for 20–30 minutes to meld the flavors in the soup. (You can also refrigerate the soup at this point and reheat it later.)

5. Meanwhile, preheat the oven to 350F/176C with the rack in the middle of the oven. Lay the baguette slices on a large baking pan. Toast the bread for about 15 minutes or until completely dry, turning each slice over once.

6. Combine the cheeses (if using more than one type) and spread the cheese mixture over the bread slices. Place the oven rack in the top third of the oven and turn on the broiler. Place the bread and cheese under the broiler and broil just long enough to melt the cheese.

7. Adjust the flavors of the soup with salt and pepper. Remember to salt this soup well. Remove bay leaves and sprigs of thyme. Ladle the soup into 6 bowls. Top each with 3 thin slices of baguette (or, one large slice).

Pho Bo
(Beef Noodle Soup)

10–12 servings

Fragrant, spicy, sweet, sour, and soothing goodness, this famous Vietnamese soup is well appreciated by many. Unfortunately, most restaurants spike it with MSG. The type of bones and the amount of each spice you use will all change the soup, and all variations are great. This version is one of my favorite ways to enjoy it, but feel free to vary the recipe according to your preferences. It's adapted from a recipe given to me by a local Asian chef and the Beef Pho recipe from Intro to the Vietnamese Kitchen by Andrea Nguyen.

I have used half oxtail to make pho for a super-rich and flavorful broth, but oxtail is very expensive (especially grass-fed), unless I have some from my "cow share." So, I have also made this with all knucklebones with great success. If you use marrowbones, don't use too many. Just a pound or two will add a lot of richness.

The black cardamom has a musty, earthy flavor that is very unique. Use five for a stronger cardamom taste and just two or three for a more subtle flavor. I have made pho without cardamom with success, but the recipe given to me by a local restaurant owner specifies that it is a vital part of pho (in her opinion). I have been able to find black cardamom at Asian markets. You can try green cardamom in its place, but the flavor will be different.

For the broth

2 medium yellow onions

3-inch/7.6-cm piece plump fresh ginger

5 pounds/2.26 kilograms knuckle bones and marrow bones (can replace half of the bones with oxtail for a very rich broth per note above)

¼ cup/38 grams whole fennel seeds

10 whole cloves

5 star anise

3 cinnamon sticks

5 black cardamom pods

1½–2 pounds/680–900 grams small flat rice noodles (bánh phở), dried (can be found at Asian markets or in the ethnic food aisle of many grocery stores)

¼ cup/60 ml fish sauce

2 tablespoons coconut sugar, whole cane sugar, or sweetener of your choice (optional)

1 pound/450 grams chuck roast, brisket, rump roast, London broil, tri-tip steak, or eye of round, etc., cut into very thin large slices across the grain*

Garnish choices

1 yellow or sweet onion, very thinly sliced

Thai basil (or sweet basil)

Fresh mint

4 cups/226 grams bean sprouts, washed

4–5 fresh limes

Several fresh Thai peppers or jalapeño peppers

---

*If you have a hard time cutting your meat thin enough and are worried that it hasn't cooked all the way through in the bowl, simply place it directly in the broth on the stove and cook for 1–3 minutes. Remove it with a slotted spoon or with a ladle and put it in a bowl. Be aware that overcooking makes meat tough.

1. Place the onions and ginger in a heavy cast-iron skillet and cook over medium heat, turning to cook evenly, for 15 minutes or until the skin of both is charred in places. (You could also put them under the broiler or hold them with tongs over a gas stove burner.)

2. Meanwhile, place the beef bones in a large pot. Cover them with water and bring to a boil. Boil for 2–3 minutes to remove impurities and make a clearer broth.

3. Carefully drain the broth through a sieve in the sink and rinse off bones with the cold water. Scrub the pot with warm water to remove any scum.

GLUTEN-FREE
DAIRY-FREE

4. Put the bones back in the pot and cover with 20 cups/4.7 liters of water. Bring the water back to a simmer and skim any further scum that rises to the top. Turn the heat down to hold the soup at a low simmer.

5. Once the onions and ginger are charred, remove them from the skillet to cool.

6. Using the same skillet, toast the fennel and cloves for 1–2 minutes or until they are very lightly browned. Stir constantly to prevent burning. Add to pot.

7. Add the star anise, cinnamon, and black cardamom to the skillet. Toast them, stirring as needed to prevent burning, until you see the cinnamon start to brown (3–5 minutes). Put the cinnamon and star anise in the pot of soup.

8. Crush the black cardamom with a meat hammer or other blunt kitchen tool. Remove the seeds and add the seeds to the pot of soup.

9. When the ginger and onions are cool enough to handle, peel both and remove the root ends of the onions with a sharp paring knife or vegetable peeler. Add the ginger and onions to the soup.

10. Simmer the soup, covered, for 3–12 hours.

11. A half hour before serving, place the thinly sliced onion in a separate bowl and cover it with cool water until serving time. You do this a half-hour before serving because that is how much time it needs to sit. (Drain it and place on the plate with herbs right before serving.)

In a large separate bowl, cover the rice noodles with cool water for 30 minutes. Wash and dry the herbs and bean sprouts. Quarter the limes and slice the hot peppers. Place all of the garnishes on a large plate for serving.

12. When the soup is done, strain it through a fine sieve into a heat-safe bowl or pot. Return the strained soup to the original pot and bring it to a low simmer. Flavor it with fish sauce to taste and/or salt and sweetener. (You can flavor it entirely with fish sauce, but it gets a little too fishy for me that way.) Take the soup right to the verge of being too salty, as the noodles will dilute some of the saltiness.

13. Fill a separate medium/large-sized pot with water and bring it to a boil for boiling the noodles. If you are serving a large crowd, you can make all of the noodles at once: Add the noodles to the pot of boiling water and cook for just 20–30 seconds or until the noodles lose their stiffness. Remove them immediately with a spider spoon, or drain in the sink over a fine sieve. If you are just making a few servings at a time, lower a portion of the noodles in a fine sieve or on a spider spoon into the boiling water for 20–30 seconds and remove. Place about a cup of noodles in each individual bowl.

14. Place a few slices of raw meat in each individual bowl on top of the noodles and pour very hot broth over them. While still quite hot, add your choice of garnishes so that the flavors infuse into the broth.

Sparkling Mint Melon Soup

12–15 small servings

116

There was a little restaurant that my husband and I liked for special dates on anniversaries and birthdays. On our first visit, we had an amazing gourmet meal, slowly brought out in stages, allowing us to savor every bite. We ended with a mint melon dessert soup that was spiked with sparkling wine and a scoop of cream. This soup is in memory of that special night. I decided to use vanilla ice cream and Prosecco, which is an Italian sparkling white wine that is less expensive than champagne. However, any favorite sparkling wine will work. If you would rather not use wine, kombucha makes a good substitute. Just note the different ratios to use. This is a great celebration dessert soup! Cut in half if not serving to a crowd.

2 cups cubed cantaloupe

2 cups cubed honeydew melon

12 medium/large spearmint leaves

2 tablespoons honey

Chilled Prosecco (sparkling wine) or kombucha

High-quality vanilla ice cream

1. In a food processor or blender, blend the cantaloupe, melon, spearmint leaves, and honey until mostly smooth with just a little bit of texture left.

2. Chill for 1–3 hours.

3. To serve, mix equal amounts of the melon soup with the sparkling wine in individual small bowls. I suggest ¼ cup/60 ml of each. Add a small scoop of ice cream to the bowl and serve right away. For the kombucha version, use 2 parts melon soup to 1 part kombucha.

Vegetarian-Friendly
GLUTEN-FREE
Grain-free

Vietnamese Hot and Sour Soup with Pineapple

6–8 servings

118

This soup is based on our favorite soup from an Asian restaurant that was just down the street from our first duplex together. It's a sweet memory from our first year of married life. It is sweet from the pineapple; hot from the peppers; and sour from the lemongrass, Kaffir lime leaves, and lime juice. We no longer live in that area, but when we get the craving, we can make our own. Be careful when touching the chili peppers. You may want to use gloves, and never touch your eyes after handling them. Serve with rice on the side if desired. Canned pineapple is fine, but use pineapple in 100 percent juice. You'll want about 3 cups of chunky pineapple for the recipe.

1 small/medium pineapple, peeled and diced (about 3 cups cubed pineapple) (save the core)	2 stalks of lemongrass, cut in half if needed to fit in the pot	1 cup thinly sliced mushrooms (your choice of variety)	1 tablespoon coconut or palm sugar (or sweetener of your choice)
4 medium shallots	½-inch/1.2-cm piece of galangal or fresh ginger, cut into thin slices, or 2 tablespoons freshly grated ginger	3 medium tomatoes, stemmed and cut into eight slices	**To Serve**
10–12 dry Thai peppers			Fresh bean sprouts
2 tablespoons fat of your choice (see page 23)		¼ cup plus 2 tablespoons/90 ml fish sauce	Thai basil or sweet basil
¾ pound/340 grams boneless, skinless chicken breasts or thighs	8 Kaffir lime leaves		Fresh mint (optional)
	2 cups sliced baby bok choy	¼ cup/60 ml plus extra fresh lime juice	Fresh cilantro (optional)
			Crumbled chili peppers (optional)

1. If you have a juicer, juice the pineapple core. If not, blend the core with a little water (if needed) in a regular blender or food processor. Strain it through a fine sieve and add water so that the mixture equals 8 cups of liquid. Set aside.

2. Place the shallots (with peel) and 6 Thai chili peppers in a small cast-iron skillet and turn on the heat to medium. Turn the chili and shallots over until the peppers are dark but not burnt. Remove the peppers and continue to cook the shallots.

3. When the peppers are cool, crumble or crush them in a mortar and pestle. Be careful not to get the chili pepper dust in the air, as it will tickle your throat.

4. Keep turning the shallots over until the peel is dark and burnt in places. Then remove them to cool. When they are cool enough to handle, peel them with a sharp knife.

5. Meanwhile, in a large pot, heat 2 tablespoons of the fat of your choice over medium heat. When hot, add 4–6 of the dried chili peppers to the oil (adjust the number of peppers based on how hot you want your soup). Sauté the peppers until they are browned and the oil is spiced. Remove the peppers and discard them.

6. Add the water/pineapple juice from the pineapple core, chicken, lemongrass, galangal or ginger, peeled shallots, Kaffir lime leaves, remaining pineapple, bok choy, mushrooms, and tomatoes to the pot and bring the soup to a boil. Turn the heat to low and simmer for 10 minutes.

7. Remove the chicken, Kaffir leaves, lemongrass, and galangal or ginger (unless grated) and set aside.

8. While the chicken is cooling, season the soup with the fish sauce, lime juice, and sugar, adding more, if desired, to taste.

9. Chop the chicken and add it back to the soup.

10. Serve the soup with the bean sprouts, basil, mint and cilantro (if using), and crumbled chili peppers for those who want it spicy.

Soups with Noodles

Noodles are a perfect addition to soup, and it's a popular addition with both children and adults. Noodles can take many forms: soft homemade noodles, fancy-shaped noodles from the store, pure white rice noodles floating in spicy broth, or thick udon noodles. You can even make your own noodles out of vegetables!

In the introduction to this book, I discussed the benefits of soaking, fermenting, or sprouting grains (pages 18–21). You can certainly make homemade noodles for the best-of-the-best nutrition. However, I do keep certain "compromise noodles" on hand. Examples include brown rice noodles in a variety of shapes (bought very cheaply at Trader Joe's) and Asian white rice noodles. The most important thing is to have a nourishing, tasty broth for both flavor and health.

Other soup recipes with noodles:

INSTRUCTIONS FOR VEGETABLE NOODLES, PAGE 35

INSTRUCTIONS FOR HOMEMADE SPROUTED EGG NOODLES, PAGE 36

CHICKEN NOODLE SOUP—THREE WAYS, PAGE 94

PHO BO, PAGE 114

Chicken Meatball Soup with Pasta and Greens

6 servings

I love this soup because it manages to be filling without being too heavy. Use whatever pasta you like, whether gluten-free or homemade. I prefer a delicate noodle in this soup. I like using the greens of radishes; they are lovely and it saves them from being wasted. You can also serve the radishes on the side. Either scrub the radishes and serve them whole, dipped in butter and unrefined salt (a delicious French custom), or serve them thinly sliced on buttered bread. You can also easily use watercress, spinach, or whatever other green catches your fancy or that you have on hand.

Make sure you use a tasty chicken stock for this recipe, as this simple soup cooks everything together in the stock without any added sautéing of vegetables. For extra flavor, consider garnishing the soup with basil or other fresh herbs or topping it with gremolata (see page 276) or pesto (see page 274). One recipe tester enjoyed this soup with red pepper flakes added to the broth and served with Parmesan cheese. Yum!

10 cups/2.3 liters chicken stock

2½ teaspoons unrefined salt (omit if using store-bought stock)

4 ounces/113 grams pasta of your choice (I used gluten-free angel hair)

1 batch chicken meatballs (see page 284)

1 bunch radish greens or other green of your choice

1. In a large pot on high heat, add the chicken stock and salt and bring it to a boil.

2. Check the package for how long your pasta takes to cook. The meatballs, when kept small, take only about 5 minutes to cook. You may need to start the pasta first and add the meatballs a few minutes into the cooking process. For the pasta I used, I was able to add them both to the pot at the same time. Drop the meatballs and pasta in at appropriate times and cook.

3. When the noodles and meatballs are cooked, add the greens and cook for several minutes or until they are wilted.

4. Salt and pepper the soup to taste and serve.

Miso Udon and Chicken Soup

4–6 servings

My family loves this soup, which is quick to throw together and very satisfying with the garlic and ginger miso broth and noodle "slurpiness." The more soy sauce you add, the saltier the soup will become, so adjust the soy sauce to taste, just like you would when salting a soup, especially if you're using a store-bought chicken stock. You can also garnish it with sliced green onions for extra crunch and a burst of flavor. It's been a favorite since I adapted it from a Williams-Sonoma recipe.

8 ounces/226 grams udon noodles (for gluten free, buy 100 percent buckwheat noodles)

8 cups/1.9 liters chicken stock

¼ cup/60 ml miso paste

1 small garlic clove, peeled and finely minced by hand or in a garlic press

2 teaspoons fresh chopped ginger

2 tablespoons soy sauce or tamari (use tamari for gluten-free option)

¾ pound/340 grams boneless skinless chicken breasts or thighs, thinly sliced or diced into bite-sized pieces or 1½ cups/210 grams leftover cooked chicken, shredded

1 bunch spinach, washed well and stemmed or 4 cups/120 grams baby spinach

1. Make the noodles according to the package directions and rinse well. Set aside.

2. In a large pot, add the chicken stock and miso paste. Whisk together.

3. Add the garlic, ginger, and soy sauce and bring the mixture to a simmer.

4. If using raw chicken, add it now and simmer it gently for 5–7 minutes or until cooked through.

5. If using leftover chicken, add it with the spinach and simmer until the spinach is wilted.

6. Add the noodles to the pot and taste-test; adjust the flavor with more soy sauce or tamari as needed.

Clam or Mussel Version

In place of raw chicken, add 1 pound/450 grams of scrubbed Manila clams (see page 222 for the care of clams). Add them to the pot in Step 3 and cook until the clams are just opened. Remove any that didn't open and proceed with Step 5 of the recipe.

Vegetarian Udon Soup with Mushrooms and Eggs

4 servings

126

I love the earthy mushroom stock combined with the flavorful ginger, garlic, and soy sauce. This makes a refreshing, yet filling meal that will please both vegetarians and omnivores.

6 cups/1.4 liters mushroom vegetable stock

¼ cup/60 ml soy sauce or tamari (use tamari for gluten-free option)

1-inch/2.5-cm fresh ginger, thinly sliced

3 garlic cloves, smashed

8–12 ounces/226–340 grams udon noodles (the larger amount will provide a pile of noodles for each bowl)

¼ pound/113 grams mushrooms of your choice (shitake are especially nice), thinly sliced

1 medium carrot, julienned (cut into matchsticks)

3 green onions, thinly sliced (root ends and top two inches discarded)

2 heaping teaspoons of wakame seaweed (optional)

4 hard boiled eggs, or Marbled Spiced Tea Eggs (see page 288)

1. In a large pot on high heat, bring the stock, soy sauce, ginger, and garlic to a boil. Turn the heat to low and simmer, covered, for 10 minutes.

2. Meanwhile, cook the udon noodles in a separate pot, according to the package directions. When done, rinse the noodles well with cold water and separate them into 4 bowls.

3. Add the mushrooms to the pot after the 10 minutes of cooking time and cook for 7–10 more minutes or until the mushrooms are well cooked.

4. Add the carrot sticks, green onions, and wakame and cook for about 3 minutes or until the carrots are soft.

5. To serve, remove the garlic and ginger (optional). Add more soy sauce, if needed, to make a saltier soup, as the saltiness will be cut down once it has been poured over the noodles.

6. Top each bowl with a hardboiled egg or Marbled Spiced Tea Egg, cut in half, and serve.

Vegetarian-
Friendly
DAIRY-FREE

Meatball and Zucchini Noodle Soup

4 servings

This soup is satisfying without grains because it uses zucchini noodles. It makes a refreshing meal that is complex in flavor due to the addition of the gremolata (don't skip it!) without a lot of ingredients. Because this soup is so simple, I especially urge you to use homemade stock; it makes all the difference. You could also substitute basil or pesto for the gremolata. Freshly shredded Parmesan makes a delicious extra garnish, if you like.

4 cups/.9 liter beef stock

Unrefined salt to taste

2 tablespoons tomato paste (I recommend Bionatura's brand, both because of flavor and quality and because it comes in a glass jar that doesn't have a "tinny" taste)

1 recipe Italian Beef Meatballs (see page 284)

4 small to medium zucchini squash, turned into fine noodles (see page 35)

1 recipe Basil Parsley Gremolata (see page 276)

1. In a large pot on low heat, bring the stock, salt, and tomato paste to a simmer.

2. Drop the meatballs into the pot and cook for 5 minutes or until the meatballs are cooked through.

3. Add the zucchini noodles and cook for 1–2 minutes or until the noodles are just cooked.

4. Add pepper and more salt to taste, if necessary. Serve with the gremolata (allowing it to steep in the soup for a minute or two before eating).

Quick Recipe
GLUTEN-FREE
Grain-free
GAPS-friendly
DAIRY-FREE
Budget-Friendly

Pho Ga
(Chicken Noodle Soup)

8 servings

I adore both types of pho, but the chicken version, in which I use spices with a lighter hand, has a milder flavor. While there are several steps to making this soup, each one is simple. I consider chicken pho easier to make than beef pho.

Once again, pho is so fun because everyone is able to flavor their bowls based on their own preferences. I find stores that carry bulk herbs and spices (such as Whole Foods) very helpful when making pho because I can buy just a small amount of each spice very cheaply.

Speaking of cheap, many recipes for chicken pho use a whole chicken! I've made it that way, and I have also made it with inexpensive drumsticks. I found that the cheap version was very tasty, and if you add the optional chicken feet, it will be quite rich, too. To add even more nutrition and flavor to the broth, you can take a cleaver knife and whack the chicken drumsticks to expose the marrow in the bones. If you don't use chicken feet, you can add chicken stock in place of part of the water.

FOR THE BROTH

1 large yellow or sweet onion

3-inch/7.6-cm piece fresh ginger

3 pounds/1.36 kilograms chicken drumsticks or legs

5 chicken feet (optional)

16 cups/3.8 liters water

1 tablespoon whole fennel

1 tablespoon whole coriander

3 cinnamon sticks

6 cloves

2 tablespoons coconut sugar, rapadura, sucanat, or other sweetener of your choice

1–1½ pounds/680–900 grams small flat rice noodles (bánh phở), dried (can be found at Asian markets or in the ethnic food aisle of many grocery stores)

2–4 tablespoons fish sauce

GARNISH CHOICES

1 yellow or sweet onion, very thinly sliced

Thai basil or sweet basil

Fresh cilantro

3 cups/170 grams bean sprouts, washed

4 limes

Several Thai peppers or jalapeño peppers

Sliced green onions

Fresh mint

1. In a heavy cast-iron skillet over medium heat, place the onion and ginger. Cook for 15 minutes, turning to cook evenly, until the skin of both the onion and ginger are charred in places. You could also put them under the broiler or hold them with tongs over a gas stove burner.

2. Meanwhile, place the chicken legs and feet in a large pot on high heat and cover with water. Bring to a boil for 2–3 minutes. (This helps remove impurities and makes a clearer broth.)

3. Carefully drain the water through a sieve in the sink and rinse the chicken with cool water. Scrub the pot with warm water to remove any scum.

4. Put the chicken back into the pot on medium heat and cover it with 16 cups/3.8 liters of water. Bring the water to a simmer and skim any further scum. Turn the heat to low and hold the soup at a low simmer.

5. When the onion and ginger are charred, remove them from the skillet to cool. Set aside.

6. Using the same skillet, toast the fennel and coriander for 1–2 minutes or until they are very lightly browned. Stir constantly to prevent burning. Then, add them to the soup pot.

7. When the ginger and onion are cool enough to handle, peel both and remove the root ends of the onion with a sharp paring knife

GLUTEN-FREE
DAIRY-FREE
Budget-Friendly

or vegetable peeler. Add them to the soup pot, along with the cinnamon, cloves, sugar (if using), and salt to taste. Simmer for 25 minutes.

8. After 25 minutes, the chicken should be cooked. Remove the drumsticks with tongs and cool. When they are cool enough to handle, remove the meat from the bones, discarding the skin. Cover the meat and refrigerate until needed.

9. Add the chicken bones back to the soup pot and continue cooking for at least 2 hours and up to 12 hours.

10. A half hour before serving, place the thinly sliced onion in a small bowl and cover it with cool water. (Drain before serving.) Cover the rice noodles with cool water in a large separate bowl. Wash and dry the herbs and bean sprouts. Quarter the limes and slice the hot peppers. Place all of these garnishes on a large plate for serving.

11. When the soup is done, strain it through a fine sieve or cheesecloth over a coarse sieve into a heat-safe bowl or pot. Return the liquid to the soup pot and shred the saved chicken meat into

it. Bring it to a low simmer and flavor it with fish sauce and/or salt to taste. (You can flavor it entirely with fish sauce, but it gets a little too fishy for me that way.) The noodles will dilute the saltiness, so add enough to make it almost too salty.

12. Fill a separate medium to large-sized pot with water and bring it to a boil for cooking the noodles. If you are serving a large crowd, you can make all of the noodles at once: Add the noodles to the pot of boiling water and cook for just 20–30 seconds or until the noodles lose their stiffness. Remove them immediately with a spider spoon or drain them in the sink over a fine sieve. If you're making just a few servings at a time, lower a portion of the noodles in a fine sieve or on a spider spoon into the boiling water for the 20–30 seconds and remove. Place the noodles in the individual serving bowls.

13. Ladle the broth with the chicken over the noodles in the bowls and serve with the plate of toppings. Everyone should add herbs, peppers, bean sprouts, drained onion, and lime juice into their individual bowls to taste.

Broth with Crepe Noodles

4–6 first-course servings

Crepes are one of the many fantastic foods from France. One traditional way to serve leftover crepes was by cutting them into noodles and serving them in a rich broth. So, the next time you make crepes, why not make an extra batch to serve the next day in a soup? Or follow the crepe recipe below to make just enough for the soup. One word about the stock/broth you use: Make sure you use a full-bodied, well-salted one, as this simple soup depends on a flavorful background. I love topping this soup with fresh herbs, such as basil, parsley, or a mixture like gremolata or pesto. To make it a full meal, add some meatballs (beef if using beef stock, chicken if using chicken stock) or leftover shredded chicken. For a vegetarian option, add cooked white beans.

6 cups/1.4 liters stock or broth of your choice

6–8 6-inch/15-cm crepes

1 bunch spinach, washed well with the stems cut off or 4 cups/120 grams baby spinach

Chopped herbs of choice or Basil Parley Gremolata (see page 276) or Delicious Pesto (see page 274)

1. In a large pot, heat the broth over high heat and add salt and pepper to taste.

2. Roll the crepes two at a time into a tight roll and slice them into thin noodles.

3. Add the noodles and spinach to the broth right before serving, cooking until the spinach is just wilted.

4. Serve the soup with your fresh herbs of choice, gremolata, or pesto.

Basic Crepe Recipe

8 6-inch/15-cm crepes

Crepes can be made with a variety of flours, including gluten-free flours like buckwheat and chestnut. Gluten-free versions will be more delicate, so be careful when flipping them. Using sprouted flour makes them more nutritious.

1 cup/140 grams flour of your choice (sprouted wheat, buckwheat, chestnut, sprouted brown rice, etc.)

1¼ cups/300 ml whole milk or Almond Milk (see page 292)

¼ teaspoon salt

2 eggs, whisked well

Butter for the pan

1. In a medium bowl, whisk together the flour, milk, salt, and eggs until the batter is smooth.

2. To remove the lumps, stir the batter through a fine sieve into a separate bowl. Let it sit, covered, for 1 hour.

3. Thin the batter with more milk, if necessary. Add one small spoonful at a time until it is the consistency of heavy cream.

4. Heat a medium saucepan over medium heat until hot and add some butter. Immediately pour 3–4 tablespoons of batter into the pan. Swirl it to coat the bottom of the pan evenly. Cook until the top appears dry and turn over. Cook until brown spots appear on the second side of the pan and turn the crepe over onto a plate. Repeat for the remaining crepes.

Quick Recipe
GLUTEN-FREE
DAIRY-FREE
Budget-Friendly

Miso Soba and Salmon Soup

4–6 servings

134

This fish-based broth is gently flavored with garlic, ginger, miso, and soy sauce. It's then beefed up with mushrooms, watercress, and salmon and served over soba noodles.

8 ounces/226 grams soba noodles

1 batch Anchovy Stock (see page 60)

1 tablespoon fresh grated ginger

3 medium garlic cloves, peeled and finely minced by hand or in a garlic press

2 tablespoons miso

1 tablespoon soy sauce or tamari, plus more to taste, if necessary (use tamari for gluten-free option)

⅓–½ pound/150–226 grams mushrooms of your choice, sliced thinly (shitake is a favorite)

½ pound/226 grams skinless, boneless wild salmon, cut into small pieces

1 bunch watercress or spinach, stems intact (trim just the very end of the stem) and washed well

1. Cook the soba noodles according to the package directions. Rinse well and divide into 4–6 individual serving bowls (4 for large servings and 6 for smaller servings).

2. In a large pot on medium heat, bring the Anchovy Stock, ginger, garlic, miso, and soy sauce to a simmer, cover, and continue to simmer for 5 minutes.

3. Add the mushrooms and cook for 4 minutes (keeping the stock at a low simmer).

4. Add the salmon and cook for another 3–4 minutes or until the salmon is just cooked through.

5. Add the watercress or spinach and cook for 1 more minute.

6. Taste test and add more soy sauce or tamari if needed.

7. Divide the soup over the noodles and serve.

Turkey Noodle Soup

8 servings

This kid-friendly soup is perfect on a cold night or when someone is under the weather. It's a forgiving recipe, so you can easily play around with substitutions as well. For example, use spinach or green beans instead of peas, or play around with seasonings. Mushrooms always pair well with turkey, and cubed and peeled sweet potatoes could add interest, too. Have fun with it!

2 tablespoons fat of your choice (see page 23)

1 large yellow onion, peeled and chopped

3 garlic cloves, peeled and finely minced by hand or in a garlic press

4 carrots, peeled and chopped

2 celery sticks, thinly sliced

10 cups/2.3 liters turkey stock

¾ teaspoon poultry seasoning or 1½ teaspoons Italian seasoning or Herbs de Provence

4 ounces/113 grams dried pasta of your choice or one Sprouted Flour Noodle recipe (see page 36). Use gluten-free rice pasta for a gluten-free soup

1½ cups/210 grams leftover roasted turkey

1 cup/150 grams frozen peas

Unrefined salt and ground pepper

1. In a large pot, heat the fat of your choice over medium to medium-high heat until hot.

2. Add the onion, garlic, carrots, and celery to the pot and sprinkle with salt. Sauté, stirring as needed to prevent burning, until the vegetables are soft.

3. Add the stock and seasonings to the pot and bring the stock to a boil. Then turn the heat to low, cover, and cook for 10 minutes.

4. Add the noodles and cook in the soup according to the time on the package directions.

5. Add the turkey and peas and heat through.

6. Salt and pepper to taste and serve.

GLUTEN-FREE
DAIRY-FREE
Budget-Friendly

Creamy Vegetable Soups

I've always loved soups that are full of vegetables. There is something about pairing a rich stock with the light vegetables that I find both satisfying and refreshing. It started with the Cream of Vegetable Soup (see page 100) and morphed in all sorts of directions from there. Pretty much any vegetable can be made into a creamed vegetable soup, so definitely use these recipes as a springboard for other delicious creations using what vegetables you have on hand.

While all of these soups are creamy, they don't necessarily get their creaminess from cream. Rich, Homemade Almond Milk (see page 292) and puréed potatoes both add dairy-free creaminess—without the cream. Simply puréeing the soup also makes it have a creamy texture, though adding a finishing touch of cream, almond milk, or crème fraîche helps too.

As you can see, I get full use out of my immersion blender in this section!

Butternut Apple Soup

4–6 servings

This simple soup often finds its way to our table during the fall. The sweetness of the apples and the zing of the ginger are a perfect complement to the butternut squash.

2 tablespoons fat of your choice (see page 23)

2 small/1 large yellow onion, peeled and chopped

3 garlic cloves, peeled and finely minced by hand or in a garlic press

1 medium butternut squash (3–4 pounds/1.36 grams), peeled, seeded, and cut into 2-inch/5-cm pieces

4 medium green apples, peeled, cored, and cubed (do this right before adding to the soup to prevent the apples from turning brown)

1 tablespoon grated fresh ginger

4–6 cups/.9–1.4 liters chicken or vegetable stock of your choice

GARNISH CHOICES

Crème fraîche (see page 282)

½ cup/50 grams toasted pumpkin seeds*

1. In a large pot, heat the fat of your choice over medium to medium-high heat until hot. Add the onions and garlic and a sprinkle of salt. Sauté, stirring frequently, until the onions have softened (5–7 minutes).

2. Add the butternut squash, apples, ginger, and stock (just enough to cover the squash). Salt with a generous sprinkle, and bring it to a simmer over high heat.

3. Lower the heat and simmer, covered, for about 20 minutes or until the squash and apples are quite soft.

4. Purée the soup using an immersion blender or by transferring the soup to a blender or food processor in small batches.

5. Salt to taste; thin with extra stock if necessary. Serve with garnishes of choice.

*To pan-toast pumpkin seeds, place the raw seeds in a dry pan over medium heat. Toast, stirring constantly, until the seeds turn a gentle brown. Remove them to a plate immediately to cool.

Simple Cream of Tomato Soup

4–6 servings

142 I experimented with a variety of tomato soups, one of which was a thick bisque. It was good, but in the end, I decided I didn't like it as much as this simple, thinner tomato soup. This version really allows the tomato flavor to shine, but is still very mild. You don't feel like you're eating spaghetti sauce! It's the perfect, real food alternative to the famous Campbell's Tomato Soup. Top it with Pan-Fried Croutons on page 282, or serve with grilled cheese or toasted and buttered bread and/or a large green salad. Another lovely idea is to place a couple of fresh basil leaves in each bowl to infuse its wonderful aroma into the soup.

2 tablespoons butter or fat of your choice (see page 23)

½ medium yellow or sweet onion, peeled and chopped

1 medium garlic clove, peeled and finely minced by hand or in a garlic press

3 cups/700 ml chopped tomatoes, fresh or canned (I prefer fresh)

2 cups/470 ml chicken or vegetable stock of your choice

½ teaspoon baking soda

2 cups/470 ml whole milk or Almond Milk (see page 292)

1. In a medium pot, heat the fat over medium to medium-high heat until hot. Add the onions and garlic and sprinkle with salt. Sauté, stirring as needed to prevent burning, until the onions are soft (5–7 minutes).

2. Add the tomatoes and cook for several minutes or until the tomatoes start to break down.

3. Add the chicken stock and sprinkle generously with salt. Simmer soup for 10 minutes.

4. Add the baking soda and milk.

5. Purée the liquid using an immersion blender, or blend in small batches in a blender or food processor.

6. Strain the soup through a fine sieve placed over a heat-safe bowl or pot, stirring and pressing on the tomato skins to remove all liquid.

7. Reheat the soup in the pot and salt to taste.

Tip: If the tomatoes you used aren't flavorful enough, add 1–4 tablespoons of tomato paste. Serve with desired toppings, grilled cheese, or toast.

Quick Recipe
Vegetarian-
Friendly
GLUTEN-FREE
Grain-free
GAPS-friendly
DAIRY-FREE
Budget-Friendly

Cream of Asparagus Soup with Gremolata

6–8 first-course servings

This elegant soup centers on asparagus, allowing its flavor to shine. Gremolata adds a refreshing flavor to brighten things up. I first started experimenting with gremolata for this recipe and have loved it ever since.

2 tablespoons fat of your choice (see page 23)

1 large yellow onion, peeled and chopped

2 garlic cloves, peeled

6 cups/1.4 liters chicken, beef, or vegetarian stock of your choice

5–6 small/medium red potatoes or 2 large baking potatoes, washed, peeled and diced

2 pounds/900 grams asparagus, washed and trimmed of any woody part of the stems and cut into 2-inch/5-cm pieces

1 batch Gremolata, Basil Parsley or all Parsley version (see page 276)

1. In a large pot, heat the fat over medium to medium-high heat until hot. Add the onion and garlic and sprinkle with salt. Sauté, stirring to prevent burning, until the vegetables soften (5–7 minutes).

2. Add the stock, potatoes, and asparagus to the pot. The stock should just cover the vegetables.

3. Season the soup with salt and pepper to taste and simmer on low heat for 20 minutes or until all of the vegetables are soft.

4. Using an immersion blender, purée the soup, or purée it in batches in a blender or food processor. Asparagus has a lot of fibers, so if you'd like to make a super smooth soup, put it through a food mill or gently stir through a fine sieve.

5. Return the soup to the pot and reheat it.

6. To serve, ladle it into serving bowls and sprinkle it with just a small amount of the gremolata on top while it is still piping hot. Let the soup rest a minute or two to blend the flavors, stir in the gremolata, and serve.

Quick Recipe
Vegetarian-
Friendly
Gluten-Free
Dairy-Free

Mexican Cauliflower Soup

6–8 Servings

146

This pure white, creamy soup is stuffed full of cauliflower and spiked with Mexican spices. It can be eaten simply or dressed up with a wide variety of toppings. My favorite includes the cilantro and crunchy corn chips for a contrast in texture. Avocado is always a pleasure, of course. If you want your soup especially spicy, feel free to up the amount of cayenne pepper. I have made this sans potatoes by including extra cauliflower (which makes it GAPS-Friendly and starch-free).

2 tablespoons fat of your choice (see page 23)

2 small/1 large yellow onion, peeled and chopped

6 medium garlic cloves, peeled and finely minced by hand or in a garlic press

8 cups/1.9 liters chicken, beef, or vegetarian stock of your choice

2 small heads cauliflower or 1 large head cauliflower, cut into florets (8–10 cups)

2 large baking potatoes or 4 medium red or yellow potatoes, peeled and diced

⅛ teaspoon cayenne pepper

2 teaspoons cumin powder

1½ teaspoons dried oregano

1–2 teaspoons salt

Topping Suggestions

Diced ripe avocado

Crumbled organic corn chips (yellow or blue)

Diced tomatoes

Fresh salsa

Sour cream or Crème Fraîche (see page 282)

Cooked and drained black beans

Several limes, cut into wedges

Half bunch of cilantro, stemmed and chopped

1. In a large pot, heat the fat of your choice over medium to medium-high heat until hot. Add the onions and garlic and sprinkle with salt. Sauté, stirring as needed to prevent browning, until the onions are softened.

2. Add the stock, cauliflower, potatoes, cayenne, cumin, oregano, and 1–2 teaspoons of salt (less if using store-bought broth). Bring the soup to a boil, turn heat to low, and cover. Cook for 20 minutes or until the cauliflower and potatoes are soft.

3. If you aren't using any extra toppings, remove about 6 florets of the cauliflower and set aside to cut into small bits to garnish the soup.

4. Using an immersion blender, blend the soup until smooth, or transfer it in small batches to a blender or food processor to purée.

5. Add salt and pepper to taste. Top with the chopped cauliflower florets or other topping(s) of your choice.

Quick Recipe
Vegetarian-
Friendly
GLUTEN-FREE
Grain-free
GAPS-friendly
DAIRY-FREE
Budget-Friendly

Garam Masala Carrot Soup

6 first-course servings or 4 large servings

148

Garam masala is a lovely spice mixture used in India, and it especially pairs well with carrots. You can finish this soup with a drizzle of coconut milk, cream, or crème fraîche, or you can serve it with lemon wedges or balsamic vinegar for a counterpoint to the soup's sweetness. You can also simply allow the tadka to stand alone as the finish to the soup. Tadka is a finishing oil or ghee with fried spices or onions and garlic. In this case, the garam masala is fried in the oil/ghee and added at the last minute for a finishing touch. Ghee is the traditional fat to use for the tadka, but coconut oil works well, too.

2 tablespoons fat of your choice (see page 23)

2 small/1 large yellow onions, peeled and chopped

8–10 medium carrots, stemmed and diced or thinly sliced

3 garlic cloves, peeled and crushed

4 cups/.9 liter chicken or vegetable stock of your choice

2 teaspoons cumin powder

½ teaspoon turmeric powder

1 tablespoon Ghee (see page 296) or coconut oil

1 scant tablespoon Garam Masala Spice Mixture (see page 276)

TOPPING/GARNISH CHOICES

¼ cup/60 ml heavy cream, full-fat coconut milk, or ½ cup/120 ml almond milk

Lemon wedges

Balsamic vinegar

1. In a medium pot, heat the fat of your choice over medium to medium-high heat until hot. Sauté the onions, carrots, and garlic with a sprinkle of salt for about 5 minutes or until the vegetables are softened, stirring to prevent burning.

2. Add the stock, cumin, and turmeric with another generous sprinkle of salt and bring the soup to a boil.

3. Turn the heat to low and simmer, covered, for 20 minutes or until the carrots are quite soft. Purée with an immersion blender, or transfer the soup to a blender or food processor to purée it in small batches.

4. Return the soup to the pot and reheat it.

5. To make the tadka, in a small separate pot or saucepan, heat the ghee or coconut oil over medium-high heat until hot. Add the garam masala and fry it for 1 minute or until the spices are fragrant. Pour it into the soup and stir.

6. If you're using a creamy addition, add it now, or provide lemon wedges or balsamic vinegar for individuals to add to their own serving bowls.

Quick Recipe
Vegetarian-
Friendly
GLUTEN-FREE
Grain-free
GAPS-friendly
DAIRY-FREE
Budget-Friendly

Stinging Nettle and Potato Soup

6–8 servings

Nettles are very nutritious and have long been prepared for medicinal uses. They were traditionally greatly appreciated, as they would be tender and green in the spring when many cupboards started to become sparse. This nettle and potato soup is a traditional Irish recipe. And, yes, the cooking process completely neutralizes their ability to sting.

If you can safely harvest your own, this soup is very inexpensive, too! Look for them in early spring and harvest the young shoots (wearing gloves). Just make sure you know what you're doing. Use gloves when handling the nettles while you prepare the soup, too. I'm able to find wild stinging nettles for sale in the spring at farmers markets and some grocery stores (look at health food stores or high-end grocers). I find this soup the most flavorful when served warm, rather than hot.

2 tablespoons fat of your choice (see page 23)

2 medium onions, peeled and chopped

3 garlic cloves, peeled and thinly sliced

3 pounds/1.3 kilograms potatoes, peeled and diced

6–8 cups stinging nettle leaves, thick stems carefully removed

8 cups/1.9 liters chicken or vegetable stock of your choice

2 tablespoons balsamic vinegar

Crème Fraîche for garnish (see page 282) (optional)

1. In a large pot, heat the fat of your choice over medium-high heat until hot. Add the onions and garlic and sprinkle with salt. Sauté, stirring as needed to prevent burning, until they start to soften (5–7 minutes).

2. Add the potatoes, nettles, and stock and generously salt (unless you are using store-bought stock).

3. Bring the soup to a boil, turn the heat to low, and cover. Simmer for about 15 minutes or until the potatoes are quite soft.

4. Purée the soup in small batches in a blender or food processor, or use an immersion blender.

5. Add balsamic vinegar to taste (start with 1 tablespoon) and add salt and pepper to taste before serving. Garnish with Crème Fraîche, if desired.

Quick Recipe
Vegetarian-
Friendly
GLUTEN-FREE
Grain-free
DAIRY-FREE
Budget-Friendly

Fresh Corn Soup

4 Servings

This is a recipe to make when you have lovely, fresh sweet corn, which provides a delightfully creamy soup. The starch in fresh corn does vary, so the thickness will also vary. I top it with a simple sauté of corn and red bell peppers, which add just the right crunch, while fresh basil adds the finishing note.

3 tablespoons butter or fat of your choice (see page 23)

1 small sweet or yellow onion, peeled and chopped

3 garlic cloves, peeled and finely minced by hand or in a garlic press

1½ cups/350 ml chicken or vegetable stock of your choice

4 cups/500 grams fresh corn, cut off the cob (save the cobs)

2 cups/470 ml whole milk or Homemade Almond Milk (see page 292)

1 red bell pepper, seeded, stemmed, and chopped

Handful of fresh basil, rolled into a cigar shape and thinly sliced or torn into small pieces

1. In a large pot, heat 2 tablespoons of butter or the fat of your choice over medium heat until hot. Add the onions and garlic and sauté until soft for 5–7 minutes, stirring as needed to prevent burning.

2. Add the stock, 3 corn cobs (snapped in half, if necessary), 3 cups/375 grams of the fresh corn, and a generous sprinkle of salt. Bring it to a simmer, turn the heat to low, and simmer for 7 minutes.

3. Remove the corn cobs and purée the liquid using an immersion blender or in batches in a blender or food processor.

4. Add 1 cup/236 ml of milk to the puréed soup.

5. Over a heat-safe bowl or other pot, strain the soup through a fine sieve, stirring gently with a wooden spoon and pressing on the solids to squeeze out all of the liquid.

6. Add another cup of milk and salt and pepper to taste.

7. In a separate medium saucepan, heat the remaining 1 tablespoon of butter or fat of your choice over medium heat until hot. Add the remaining cup of corn and red bell pepper and sprinkle with salt. Sauté until soft (3–5 minutes), stirring as needed to prevent burning.

8. Toss the corn and bell pepper with the basil, top the soup with the mixture, and serve.

Quick Recipe
Vegetarian-
Friendly
GLUTEN-FREE
Grain-free
DAIRY-FREE
Budget-Friendly

Roasted Garlic and Potato Soup

6–8 servings

154

Roasting garlic tames it into a smooth, flavorful bulb of goodness. While this soup contains 4 whole heads of garlic, it is mild because of the roasting process. And since the oven is on anyways while we roast the garlic, I roast half of the potatoes too for even more flavor. Use the sausage to make it into a main dish soup. This is the perfect dish to enjoy on a cold, blustery night.

4 whole heads of garlic

Drizzle of olive oil, salt, and pepper

8–10 medium red potatoes

2 tablespoons fat of your choice, plus extra for sautéing sausage (see page 23)

2 teaspoons finely minced dried rosemary or 1 tablespoon fresh, finely minced rosemary

6 cups/1.4 liters chicken, beef, or vegetarian stock of your choice

4 mild Italian sausages or bratwurst, thinly sliced (optional, leave out sausage for a vegetarian meal)

Fresh minced parsley (optional)

1. Preheat the oven to 400F/205C.

2. Remove any extra garlic skins from the heads of garlic. Using a sharp knife, cut off the top ½-inch/1.2-cm or so of each garlic head to expose each clove. Drizzle a bit of olive oil over each head and sprinkle them with salt and pepper.

3. Place the garlic in a small ovenproof pan and cover it tightly with foil. (Try to avoid the foil touching the garlic.)

4. Peel half of the potatoes and dice them. Scrub the remaining potatoes and dice them. Toss each pile of potatoes with 1 tablespoon of fat and rosemary. Lay on a sheet pan, not mixing the two types of potatoes. Place the pan in the middle of the oven along with the garlic. Roast for about 45 minutes or until the potatoes are browning. Remove the potatoes from the oven and set aside.

5. Check on the garlic by poking it with a butter knife. It is done when it's soft and smooth. It generally needs 15–30 more minutes in the oven after the potatoes have been removed. When done, remove the garlic from the oven and cool.

6. When the garlic is cool enough to handle, remove it from its papery shell by either gently squeezing the bulbs by the root end or using a small spoon to scoop out the softened garlic. Just make sure you pick out any papery skins before adding it to the soup.

7. In a large pot, add the chicken broth, peeled potatoes, garlic, and a generous sprinkle of salt. Bring the liquid to a simmer over high heat.

8. Blend the soup with an immersion blender until smooth, or transfer it to a blender or food processor in small batches and add back to pot.

9. Add the roasted unpeeled potatoes to the puréed soup.

10. In a small separate pan, heat a little bit of fat/oil and sauté the thinly sliced sausages until cooked and heated through. Add the sausage to the soup, season it with plenty of salt and pepper, as needed, and serve. Top it with the parsley (if using).

Vegetarian-
Friendly
GLUTEN-FREE
Grain-free
DAIRY-FREE
Budget-Friendly

(Dark) Green Soup

8 servings

This soup is dark and plump with greens. It's a nourishing and calcium rich, smooth soup made thicker by the addition of a small amount of rice or potato. Several of my recipe testers commented that they like this soup thicker instead of thin. In that case, you can double or even triple the amount of potatoes or rice you include. I was also told that quinoa works well, too. This soup is for greens lovers only, and don't skip the cream, as it is essential.

2 tablespoons fat of your choice (see page 23)

2 small/1 large yellow onion, peeled and chopped

4 garlic cloves, peeled and finely minced by hand or in a garlic press

1 bunch kale, preferably lacinato, well washed

8 cups/1.9 liters chicken, beef, or vegetable stock of your choice

¼ cup/45 grams white rice or 1 large potato, peeled and cubed

1½ teaspoons dried thyme

Pinch or two of cayenne pepper

1 bunch spinach, well washed to remove any grit, with the very bottom of the stems trimmed

½ cup/120 ml heavy cream or Homemade Almond Milk (see page 292)

¼ cup/60 ml freshly squeezed lemon juice

1. In a large pot heat the fat over medium high heat, until hot, but never smoking. Add the onions and garlic and sprinkle with salt. Sauté, stirring as needed to prevent burning, until the onions are soft (5-7 minutes).

2. Meanwhile prepare the kale. If you are using lacinato kale you can simply cut into 1-inch pieces. For other kale varieties, cut out the rib by folding the kale in half, and slice the stem out. Then, proceed to cut the kale into 1-inch pieces.

3. Add the rice or potato, kale, thyme and cayenne to the pot along with the broth. Bring to a boil over high heat, turn down heat, and simmer for 15 minutes. Add the spinach. It will probably be above the broth line, but as it wilts, you can push it down into the soup. Cook until soft, about 5 minutes. Add heavy cream or almond milk, and salt well. Add lemon juice, adding in tablespoon at a time, until it reaches desired flavor and then salt and pepper to taste.

Soups Centered on Legumes and Grains

Soups hearty with grains and legumes have a good fill factor and are quite delectable, too. Grains and legumes have been used in soups since the birth of agriculture, and they're a frugal choice.

I talked in the introduction of this cookbook about soaking grains and legumes (pages 18–21), and I have chosen to keep things simple by just soaking them in warm water. You can also add a kombu strip (a type of seaweed) that adds minerals and helps make legumes more digestible.

There is a debate about when to salt a legume-based soup. Traditionally, they were salted at the end of the cooking time so that the beans wouldn't "seize up" and stay hard. The current thinking is that this is an old wives' tale, but I've had some soups take a long time to cook when salted early in the cooking process. So, I'm cautious with my salt and wait until the end.

For grains, I have also tried to keep things simple when soaking, and I sometimes use white rice when I don't have time to soak brown rice (see page 21 for more on the debate about brown versus white rice). So, you can easily prepare these soups with unsoaked grains. You just need to add a little extra liquid to some of the recipes to make sure they don't get too thick. I enjoy them soaked, as they are a bit softer in texture, more nutritious, and easier to digest after a soaking period.

Other soups with grains and legumes:

German Lentil Soup, page 108

Scotch Broth, page 200

Turkey and Wild Rice Soup, page 202

Jamaican Oxtail Soup, page 218

Grain Porridges and Congees, pages 239-255

Egyptian Red Lentil Soup with Caramelized Onions

4–6 servings

160

This gentle, cumin-scented soup is topped with sweet caramelized onions, a drizzle of high-quality olive oil, and a blast of fresh lemon juice. It's incredibly easy and surprisingly delicious considering how inexpensive it is to make. You don't have to soak lentils because they are lower in phytic acid, but you're welcome to soak your lentils in warm water for 8 to 18 hours.

2½ cups/1 pound/450 grams red lentils (the orange ones, which indicates that they have been hulled)

8 cups/1.9 liters filtered water or broth of your choice (I prefer water to allow other flavors to shine)

1 medium/large yellow onion, peeled and chopped

3–6 medium garlic cloves, peeled and finely minced by hand or in a garlic press

2 teaspoons cumin

Caramelized Onions (see below)

Extra-virgin olive oil for drizzling

2 lemons, cut into wedges

1. In a large pot, add the red lentils, broth or water, onion, garlic, and cumin. Bring the soup to a boil over high heat. Turn the heat to low and simmer for 30 minutes or until the lentils and vegetables are soft.

2. Meanwhile, make the Caramelized Onions.

3. When the soup is done, you can purée it for a super smooth soup or leave it slightly textured (the lentils turn to mush when cooked).

4. Salt to taste and serve each bowl topped with a spoonful of Caramelized Onions, a drizzle of fruity olive oil, and a generous squeeze of lemon juice. I allow people to top their own soup as desired.

Caramelized Onions

2 medium/large yellow or sweet onions, peeled and thinly sliced

2 tablespoons fat of your choice (see page 23)

Salt

1. In a large saucepan, heat the fat of your choice over medium heat. Add the onions and sprinkle them generously with salt. Stir as needed to prevent premature browning, allowing the onions to "sweat" and wilt.

2. Continue to cook until the onions turn a light brown color, are sweet, and are very soft. This process takes about 30 minutes.

Quick Recipe
Vegetarian-
Friendly
GLUTEN-FREE
GAPS-friendly
DAIRY-FREE
Budget-Friendly

Mexican Black Bean Soup

4–6 servings

This flavorful, protein-rich soup is a frugal favorite. If you don't have chipotle flakes, you can substitute red pepper flakes, though it won't have quite the same smoky flavor. You can use whatever toppings you like on this soup—use them all, or use none!

2 tablespoons fat of your choice (see page 23)

1 large yellow onion, peeled and diced

1 red bell pepper, seeded, stemmed, and chopped

3–6 garlic cloves, peeled and finely minced by hand or in a garlic press

8 cups/1.9 liters filtered water or stock of your choice

1½ teaspoons dried oregano

1½ teaspoons cumin

½–1 teaspoon dried chipotle flakes (½ teaspoon for a milder soup)

2 cups/1 pound/450 grams black beans, soaked overnight or up to 24 hours in plenty of warm water, rinsed and drained

¼ cup/60 ml fresh lime juice

TOPPING CHOICES

Sour cream

Cubed avocado

Chopped cilantro

Salsa

Tortilla chips

Lime wedges

1. In a large pot, heat the fat of your choice over medium to medium-high heat. Add the onion, red bell pepper, and garlic cloves. Cook for 5 minutes or until the vegetables are soft, stirring as needed to prevent burning.

2. Add the water/stock, oregano, cumin, chipotle flakes, and soaked and rinsed black beans. Bring the soup to a boil and turn the heat to low. Skim off any scum and cover. Cook the soup until the beans are quite soft (1½–2 hours).

3. When the beans are done, salt the soup well (start with 2 teaspoons). Add lime juice to taste (start with 2 tablespoons).

4. Serve with your choice of toppings.

Vegetarian-Friendly
GLUTEN-FREE
Grain-free
DAIRY-FREE
Budget-Friendly

Fava Bean and Vegetable Soup with Pesto

4 servings

164

Fresh fava beans are a spring specialty and have a sweet, yet meaty, flavor. In this version, they are paired with vegetables and topped with flavorful pesto. While fava beans take a bit of time to prepare, we find this recipe well worth the trouble. You can find fava beans at some grocery stores and farmers markets during the spring.

2 tablespoons fat of your choice (see page 23)

1 medium yellow onion, peeled and chopped

4 carrots, peeled and diced

4 celery sticks, diced

3 garlic cloves, peeled and finely minced by hand or in a garlic press

4 cups/.9 liter chicken or light vegetable stock

2 cups shelled, fresh fava beans (3 pounds/1.3 kg unshelled fava beans) (see page 37 for shelling instructions)

TO SERVE

1 recipe Delicious Pesto (see page 274)

1. In a medium/large pot, heat the fat of your choice over medium to medium-high heat. Add the vegetables, sprinkle them with salt, and sauté them until soft (5–7 minutes).

2. Add the stock, prepared fava beans, and a generous sprinkle of salt. Bring the soup to a boil, turn the heat to low, cover, and cook at a low simmer for 15 minutes or until the vegetables are soft.

3. Salt and pepper to taste and top each bowl generously with pesto.

Easy Chicken and Rice Soup

6–8 servings

Chicken and rice soup is a gentle favorite. This version allows you to start without premade broth, which makes it easy to throw together. I've found that when using white rice, it's best to use a little less because it expands more rapidly in the broth. If you want a thicker soup, increase both the brown rice and the white rice amounts by ¼ cup/50 grams. To make a very flavorful and nutritious soup, you can replace all or some of the water with chicken stock.

1 cup/175 grams long-grain brown rice or ¾ cup/135 grams long-grain white rice

1 cup/236 ml warm filtered water (if using brown rice)

1 tablespoon kefir, yogurt, whey, kombucha, raw apple cider vinegar, or other live-culture addition (if using brown rice)

2 tablespoons fat of your choice (see page 23)

1 large/2 small yellow onions, peeled and chopped

4 medium carrots, peeled and sliced diagonally into 1-inch/2.5-cm pieces

2–4 celery sticks, sliced diagonally into 1-inch/2.5-cm pieces

3 medium garlic cloves, peeled and finely minced by hand or in a garlic press

10 cups/2.3 liters filtered water

1½–2 pounds/680–900 grams chicken drumsticks or whole chicken legs

1½ teaspoons dried (not ground) thyme

2 bay leaves

2 teaspoons unrefined salt and freshly ground pepper

Fresh minced parsley for garnish (optional)

1. In a nonreactive bowl, place the rice, warm water, and live-culture addition. Cover the bowl and leave it in a warm place for 12–24 hours. When the time has passed, drain the water and rinse the rice well. (Skip this step if you're using white rice.)

2. In a large pot, heat the fat of your choice over medium-high heat but not until smoking. Add the onions, carrots, celery, and garlic. Sprinkle the mixture with salt and sauté, stirring as needed, for 5–7 minutes or until the vegetables start to soften.

3. Add 10 cups/2.3 liters of filtered water, chicken, thyme, bay leaves, and rinsed brown rice to the pot.

4. Add 2 teaspoons of salt and a generous sprinkle of freshly ground pepper. Cover the pot and bring the soup to a simmer. Turn the heat to low and simmer, covered, for 1 hour.

5. Remove the bay leaves and chicken legs/drumsticks from the pot and let the chicken cool. When cool enough to touch, remove the skin from the chicken and shred the chicken meat, making sure there are no bones in the shredded meat. Return the meat to the pot and add more salt and pepper to taste if needed.

6. Garnish the soup with fresh minced parsley, if desired, and serve. Save the chicken bones for making into stock.

GLUTEN-FREE
DAIRY-FREE
Budget-Friendly

◦⟶ *White Rice Version* ⟵◦

Leave the rice out of the pot until after the first hour of cooking time. Remove the meat and while the chicken is cooling, add the white rice (long or short grain). Cook the soup with the rice for another 20 minutes and return the cooled meat to the pot. Season to taste.

Buckwheat and Root Vegetable Soup with Meatballs

6–8 Servings

168 This hearty soup is a favorite. It is filling without being heavy and I love how it stretches out one pound of meat. Buckwheat is a very nutritious, gluten-free grain-like seed and an ingredient in many traditional Russian dishes. It's a good source of tryptophan, an amino acid needed for a variety of body functions that helps regulate appetite, helps you sleep, and elevates your mood. It also contains magnesium and manganese, essential minerals that we are often deficient in. To fully utilize all of the nutrition in the buckwheat, I soak it overnight, but it would work easily without the soaking period or with sprouted buckwheat instead.

¾ cup/130 grams hulled buckwheat

1 cup/236 ml warm filtered water

1 tablespoon raw apple cider vinegar, yogurt, kefir, kombucha or other live-culture addition

2 tablespoons fat of your choice (see page 23)

1 large yellow or sweet onion, peeled and chopped

2 celery sticks, thinly sliced

4 large or 6 medium carrots, diced or thinly sliced

3 garlic cloves, peeled and finely minced by hand or in a garlic press

6 cups/1.4 liters beef stock

1½ teaspoons dried (not ground) thyme

2 bay leaves

1 rutabaga, peeled and diced (optional; you can substitute a turnip or other root vegetable)

6–8 red potatoes, scrubbed and diced (peel if there is any green under the skin)

1 batch Italian Beef Meatballs (see page 284)

Handful chopped parsley

1. In a large bowl, combine the buckwheat, water, and live-culture addition. Cover the bowl and leave it in a warm place for 12 to 24 hours. Drain and rinse the buckwheat well through a fine sieve before adding to the soup.

2. In a large pot, heat the fat of your choice over medium to medium-high heat. Add the onion, celery, carrots, and garlic. Sprinkle with salt and sauté for five minutes or until the vegetables start to get soft. Stir as needed to prevent burning.

3. Add the stock, thyme, bay leaves, rutabaga, potatoes, and buckwheat. Salt to taste. Bring the soup to a boil, turn the heat to low, cover, and simmer for 15 minutes or until the buckwheat and root vegetables are fully cooked.

4. Add the meatballs and cook for 5 minutes or until they are cooked through.

5. Salt and pepper to taste and add a generous handful of chopped parsley right before serving.

Chicken Version

Replace the beef stock and meatballs with chicken stock and Chicken Meatballs (see page 284).

Simple Lentil Soup

4–6 servings

This is the simplest of soups, so I often make it weekly. In this recipe, I don't even sauté the vegetables! While perhaps too simple for some, I love it, and so does my five-year-old. My husband says it would be even better with some crispy bacon sprinkled on it or pan-fried ham. These can certainly be added for the meat lovers. Another delicious way to enjoy this soup is by adding cheesy toast into it.

2¼ cups/1 pound/450 grams green or brown lentils, soaked overnight in warm water (optional), drained, and rinsed

6 cups/1.4 liters chicken, beef, or vegetable stock (or combination of water and broth)

1 small yellow onion, peeled and cut in half

3 garlic cloves, peeled

2 bay leaves

⅛ teaspoon powdered cloves

1½ teaspoons dried (not ground) thyme, Herbes de Provence, or Italian herb mixture

1 strip of kombu (optional; don't use for GAPS Friendly)

1–2 tablespoons balsamic vinegar (optional; don't use for GAPS Friendly. Can use lemon juice instead.)

1. Place the lentils and the rest of the ingredients, except the balsamic vinegar, in a medium-sized pot. Bring the soup to a simmer over high heat.

2. Turn the heat to low and cover the pot. Cook for 45 to 60 minutes or until the lentils are soft. If you didn't soak the lentils, you will need to add up to 2 cups/470 ml more water. If at any time the liquid gets too low, add more to keep the lentils covered throughout the cooking process.

3. Remove the kombu strip and bay leaves from the pot.

4. Purée the soup with an immersion blender, or transfer it to a blender or food processor in small amounts.

5. Season the soup generously with unrefined salt and freshly ground pepper. Add the balsamic vinegar (if using), starting with 1 tablespoon. Taste; add more if preferred. Serve with desired toppings.

Topping choices

Spoonful of Crème Fraîche (see page 282) or natural sour cream on each serving bowl

Fresh herbs, such as thyme, parsley, or basil, sprinkled on top

Grated Parmesan cheese

Spoonful of Dijon-style mustard

Poached egg

Pan-Fried Croutons (see page 282)

Quick Recipe
Vegetarian-
Friendly
GLUTEN-FREE
GAPS-friendly
DAIRY-FREE
Budget-Friendly

Simple Split Pea Soup

6–8 servings

I've always loved pea soup. It's smooth and thick at the same time with that earthy legume flavor I love. I like to add carrots to sweeten it, and a ham bone or smoked ham hock is delicious in the soup, although the vegetarian version is also great. If you want a smoky flavor without ham, consider adding a bit of smoked salmon to the pot during cooking and top each bowl with more of the salmon. Or sprinkle a bit of naturally smoked sea salt over each bowl of soup for a subtle smokiness!

2 tablespoons fat of your choice (see page 23)

1 large or two small onions, peeled and chopped

4 medium carrots, peeled and diced

2 celery sticks, washed, trimmed, and diced

3 garlic cloves, peeled and finely minced by hand or in a garlic press

1½ teaspoons dried (not ground) thyme

1 teaspoon dried marjoram

2 bay leaves

8 cups/1.9 liters filtered water or chicken, beef, or vegetable stock

2¼ cups/1 pound/450 grams split peas, soaked overnight in plenty of warm water in a warm place, and rinsed

1. In a large pot, add the fat of your choice and heat until hot. Add the onions, carrots, celery, and garlic. Sauté, stirring frequently, for 5–7 minutes, or until the vegetables start to soften.

2. Add the herbs, bay leaves, water, and rinsed split peas. Bring the soup to a boil. Then, turn the heat to low to keep it at a simmer for 40 minutes or until the peas are quite soft.

3. Remove the bay leaves.

4. Purée the soup using an immersion blender or a regular blender or food processor in small batches to avoid splattering the hot liquid. If you prefer more texture, leave it partially un-puréed. Thin with broth/water if desired.

5. Salt to taste, starting with 2 teaspoons of unrefined salt. Add pepper to taste and serve.

Ham Hock Version

Add 1 ham hock along with the split peas and the rest of the ingredients. Remove the ham to cool it before puréeing the soup. If there is any meat on the ham hock, shred it and add it back to the soup after the puréeing process.

Quick Recipe
Vegetarian-
Friendly
GLUTEN-FREE
Grain-free
DAIRY-FREE
Budget-Friendly

Cock-a-Leekie

6–8 servings

This soup has quite the history. Generally considered a Scottish recipe (though other European countries have similar recipes), it's a filling version of chicken and rice soup that goes back to the Medieval Ages. What makes it special is the prunes. I know that the word "prune" has been demonized, so if it helps, think of them as "dried plums." They give this soup its subtle sweetness, and my children especially like it! It's unfortunate that most modern versions of this soup leave the prunes out because they're what make it so unique. I didn't want the sweetness to overwhelm, though, so I decided to add bacon for a salty counterpart. You could certainly just make sure to salt the soup well instead, but we especially enjoy the bacon mixed with the sweet prunes as a topping.

This soup makes its own stock while it cooks, but to make it even more flavorful and nutritious, you can use chicken stock or partial chicken stock instead of the water. You can also use white rice instead of brown and skip the soaking process. The leeks add a special flavor and are traditional in the Scottish version, but if you prefer, you can substitute onions.

¾ cup/160 ml long-grain brown rice

1 cup/236 ml warm filtered water

1 tablespoon raw apple cider vinegar, kefir, yogurt, or other live-culture acidic addition

6 bacon slices

1 large/2 small yellow onions, peeled and chopped

3 medium carrots, peeled and diced

2 celery sticks, diced or thinly sliced

2 medium leeks, thinly sliced (see page 33 for instructions)

½ cup/70 grams prunes

1½ teaspoons dried (not ground) thyme

2 bay leaves

8 cups/1.9 liters filtered water or chicken stock (or a combination of water and stock)

½ pound/450 grams chicken thighs or breasts or 1½ pounds/680 grams chicken drumsticks

1½ teaspoons unrefined salt

5 prunes, diced

1. Combine the brown rice with the water and raw apple cider vinegar in a large bowl. Cover and leave the bowl in a warm room for 12–24 hours. After the time has passed, drain the rice and rinse it well.

2. In a large pot over medium heat, cook the bacon until crispy, turning as needed to cook evenly. Remove the bacon from the pot. Drain on a paper towel–lined plate and refrigerate until needed. If there is a lot of bacon grease, drain the extra, leaving 2 tablespoons behind in the pot.

3. Sauté the onions, carrots, celery, and leeks in the bacon grease over medium to medium-high heat, stirring as needed to prevent burning, for 5–7 minutes.

4. Once the vegetables start to soften, add the ½ cup/70 grams of prunes, the thyme, bay leaves, water or chicken stock,

GLUTEN-FREE
DAIRY-FREE
Budget-Friendly

chicken, 1½ teaspoons of salt, and soaked brown rice to the pot. (If you're using white rice, add it halfway through the cooking time.) Bring the soup to a boil, turn the heat to low, cover, and simmer for about 45 minutes or until the rice is cooked through.

5. Remove and discard the bay leaves and the cooked prunes (which will be quite soft).

6. Remove the chicken from the soup. If you're using chicken thighs or breasts, chop the meat when the chicken is cool enough to handle. If you're using drumsticks, remove the skin and pull the meat off of the bone. Shred the meat and save the bones for making chicken stock. Return the chicken back to the soup.

7. Salt and pepper the soup to taste.

8. Crumble the reserved bacon in a small bowl and mix it with the chopped prunes. Allow everyone to top their bowl with the bacon and prunes mixture.

Garlicky White Bean Soup with Dark Greens

10–12 servings

Something about the simplicity of this soup touches me. That you can start with just a few ingredients and make it into something so hearty and filling is a welcome change from complex recipes. You can serve it with a sprinkle of Parmesan cheese on top and rustic bread on the side.

4⅔ cups/2 pounds/.9 kilograms white beans (use white navy beans for GAPS Friendly)

12 cups/2.8 liters filtered water or homemade, unsalted stock/ broth of your choice

2 garlic cloves, smashed and peeled

3 bay leaves

¼ cup/60 ml olive oil + 2 tablespoons olive oil

4 cups/120 grams baby spinach (or one bunch of kale, Swiss chard, or other dark green)

¼ cup/60 ml tomato paste

3 teaspoons dried oregano

6 garlic cloves, peeled and minced (but not too finely)

Unrefined salt and freshly ground pepper

1. Soak the beans in a large bowl filled with warm water. Cover the bowl and set it in a warm place to soak overnight for 12 to 24 hours.

2. Rinse and drain the beans and add them to a large pot.

3. Add the water, the smashed garlic, bay leaves, and 2 tablespoons of the olive oil to the pot.

4. Bring the soup to a boil and turn the heat to low. Simmer the soup until the beans are soft and tender. How long this takes will depend on the age and type of the beans, but it should take about 1½ hours.

5. Wash and drain the baby spinach leaves, or wash and chop the greens you're using (stem kale, if using). Add the greens to the soup and simmer for a few minutes. Baby spinach will cook fast, while kale or Swiss chard can take up to 10 minutes to soften.

6. In a small saucepan, heat ¼ cup of olive oil over medium heat until hot but never smoking. Add the tomato paste, oregano, and 6 garlic cloves. Continually stir until the olive oil is tinted with red and the garlic has softened but not turned brown. Pour this mixture over the beans in the pot and stir.

7. Add plenty of salt and pepper to taste.

8. Serve slightly cooled. If you serve it piping hot, you won't be able to taste the flavors as well.

Vegetarian-Friendly
GLUTEN-FREE
GAPS-friendly
DAIRY-FREE
Budget-Friendly

French Lentil and Vegetable Soup with Pesto

8–10 servings

178

Pesto makes this lentil soup leap to new heights. There is nothing like the slow flavors of the long-simmered and the bright taste of fresh pesto married in a soup. The soaking period of the lentils is optional.

2 tablespoons fat of your choice (see page 23)

2 small/1 large yellow onions, peeled and chopped

6 carrots, peeled and thinly sliced

6 celery sticks, thinly sliced

2 large leeks, well washed and sliced into ¼-inch pieces (see page 33)

3 cloves garlic, peeled and finely minced

12 cups/2.8 liters chicken stock, vegetable broth, water, or a combination

1½ teaspoons dried (not ground) thyme or 2 sprigs fresh thyme

2 bay leaves

2¼ cups/1 pound/ 450 grams French lentils, soaked for 12–24 hours in warm water, rinsed, and drained

4 medium zucchini squash, diced

½–¾ pound/226–340 grams fresh green beans, stemmed

¼ cup/60 ml tomato paste

Half bunch parsley, chopped (optional)

1 Delicious Pesto recipe (see page 274)

1. In a large pot, heat the fat of your choice over medium to medium-high heat. Add the onions, carrots, celery, leeks, and garlic. Sauté for 5 minutes, stirring as needed to prevent burning.

2. Add the chicken stock or water, thyme, bay leaves, and lentils. Bring the soup to a boil, turn the heat to low, and simmer for 45 minutes or until the lentils are soft but not falling apart. You may need to add more liquid if you didn't soak the lentils.

3. Add the zucchini squash, green beans, and tomato paste and return the soup to a simmer for 7 more minutes.

4. Salt and pepper to taste. Add the chopped parsley (if using).

5. Serve with pesto dolloped on top of each bowl of soup.

Vegetarian-
Friendly
GLUTEN-FREE
Grain-free
GAPS-friendly
DAIRY-FREE
Budget-Friendly

Quinoa and Chicken Soup

6 servings

This recipe has been a long-time favorite of my family's plus a popular recipe on my blog. It's simple, yet has lots of flavor. The white wine is optional but is a tasty addition. You can make it with premade broth and leftover chicken, or you can make a broth during a longer cooking time by adding chicken legs into the soup. You can also throw everything into a slow cooker for several hours on high.

1 cup/½ pound/226 grams quinoa

1 cup/236 ml warm filtered water

1 tablespoons raw apple cider vinegar, kefir, yogurt, or other live-culture addition

2 tablespoons fat of your choice (see page 23)

1 medium yellow onion, peeled and chopped

4 carrots, peeled and diced or thinly sliced

2 celery sticks, thinly sliced

3 garlic cloves, peeled and finely minced by hand or in a garlic press

½–1 cup/120–236 ml white wine (½ cup for a mild wine flavor)

6 cups/1.4 liters chicken stock or water or a combination, if using chicken legs

1 teaspoon dried (not ground) thyme

2 bay leaves

1½ pounds/680 grams chicken legs or 2 cups/280grams leftover chicken meat

Fresh, chopped parsley, basil, or herb of your choice

1. In a small, nonreactive bowl, combine the quinoa, warm water, and live-culture addition. Cover the bowl and leave it in a warm place for 12–24 hours. After the time has passed, rinse the quinoa well through a fine sieve.

2. In a large pot, heat the fat of your choice over medium to medium-high heat. Add the onion, carrots, celery, and garlic and sprinkle them with salt. Sauté the vegetables for 5–7 minutes or until they start to soften.

3. Add the wine, stock/water, thyme, bay leaves, chicken legs (if using), and rinsed quinoa. Bring the soup to a boil, turn the heat to low, and cover. If using chicken legs, cook for 45 minutes to 1 hour. If using precooked meat, cook for 20 minutes, and then add the precooked chicken and cook until heated through.

4. Garnish with the herb of your choice; salt and pepper to taste.

Moroccan Fava and Vegetable Soup

4 servings

182 | This soup pairs fresh fava beans with a lot of vegetables, cumin, and turmeric. Fresh lemon juice and cilantro is used to liven it up even more. You can purée it smooth or just purée part of it for a thicker soup. In the picture, you can see both the chunky and puréed versions.

2 tablespoons olive oil or fat of your choice (olive oil would be traditional but is not as heat safe as some other fats; see page 23 for more information)

2 large leeks, thinly sliced (see page 33 for instructions)

4 carrots, peeled and thinly sliced

2 celery sticks, thinly sliced

6 cloves garlic, peeled and finely minced by hand or in a garlic press

4 cups/.9 liter chicken stock or vegetable broth

2 cups shelled, fresh fava beans (about 3 pounds/1.3 kilograms unshelled fava beans; see page 37 for shelling instructions)

1½ teaspoons ground cumin

½ teaspoon turmeric

2–4 tablespoons fresh lemon juice

Unrefined salt

Chopped cilantro (optional)

Lemon wedges (optional)

1. In a large pot, heat the oil or fat of your choice over medium to medium-high heat until just hot but never smoking. Add the leeks, carrots, celery, and garlic to the pot and sprinkle them with salt. Sauté until soft 5–7 minutes, stirring as needed to prevent browning or burning.

2. Add the stock, fava beans, cumin, and turmeric. Bring the soup to a boil, turn the heat to low, cover, and simmer for 15 minutes or until the vegetables are tender.

3. If desired, purée all or part of the soup using an immersion blender, or transfer it in small batches to a food processor or blender.

4. Add lemon juice and salt to taste, balancing the salty and sour flavors.

5. Serve with cilantro and lemon wedges if desired.

Vegetarian-
Friendly
GLUTEN-FREE
Grain-free
DAIRY-FREE

Smokey Lentil and Chicken Soup with Dark Greens

6–8 servings

184

A smoked ham hock permeates this soup, and the dark greens, tomatoes, and lentils all complement that smoky flavor. It's even tastier the next day! Soaking the lentils is optional.

2 tablespoons fat of your choice (see page 23)

1 medium yellow onion, peeled and chopped

4 carrots, peeled and diced or thinly sliced

4 celery sticks, thinly sliced or diced

3 garlic cloves, peeled and finely minced by hand or in a garlic press

1½ cups/300 grams brown lentils, soaked for 12–24 hours in warm water, rinsed, and drained

3–4 chicken drumsticks (about 1 pound/450 grams)

8 cups/1.9 liters filtered water or chicken stock or a combination

1 ham hock

14–28 ounces/414–828 ml chopped canned tomatoes (both can sizes work in this recipe)

1 bunch of kale, center rib removed and chopped into ½-inch/1.3-cm slices

Half bunch of parsley, chopped (optional)

1. In a large pot, heat the fat of your choice over medium to medium-high heat until hot but never smoking. Add the onion, carrots, celery, and garlic and sauté for 5 minutes.

2. Add the lentils, drumsticks, water or stock, and the ham hock to the pot. Bring the soup to a boil, turn the heat to low, and simmer the soup for 45 minutes or until the lentils are soft but not falling apart.

3. Remove the chicken and ham hock. When they are cool enough to handle, remove the skin from the chicken and shred the meat from the drumsticks and ham hock. The bones can be saved for making more chicken stock.

4. Return the meat to the pot.

5. Add the tomatoes and kale to the pot and return the soup to a simmer for 7 minutes or until the kale is soft.

6. Salt and pepper the soup to taste. Sprinkle with parsley (if using) and serve. This soup is even better the next day.

Hearty Soups and Stews

*T*he following recipes are especially hearty fare—either a thick soup or a stew. What is the definition of a stew, and how is it different from a soup? One difference is that a stew generally has a longer cooking time to allow its ingredients to "stew" in the pot. We often think of stews as thicker, too, although that isn't always the case.

Stews are generally chunky since they are "stewed" for longer periods of time and also often contain rich ingredients such as coconut milk or butter, which we crave more in the cold winter months. Along with the stews in this section, you'll find a variety of hearty soups that will stick to your bones, comfort you in the cold, and fill you up.

Many other recipes in this book are hearty as well, such as the grain and legume recipes, grain porridges, congees, and many of the noodle soups.

Curried Beef Stew

4–6 servings, more when served over rice

Beef stew lends itself beautifully to curry. I really don't know why I didn't think of it before. It's now a family favorite, especially when served over bowls of rice. I don't thicken this stew at all, but if you let it sit overnight in the refrigerator, it will naturally thicken as the potatoes break down. My secret is using both curry powder and garam masala for a fuller spice profile. I love the combination.

1½–2½ pounds/680–900 grams stew meat, cut into 2-inch/5-cm cubes (both amounts work, depending on how meaty you want your stew)

2 tablespoons fat of your choice (see page 23)

2 small/1 large yellow onions, peeled and chopped

1½ tablespoons curry (mild or hot)

1 heaping tablespoon garam masala

1 heaping tablespoon fresh ginger, peeled and finely shredded

3 large cloves garlic, peeled and finely minced by hand or in a garlic press

2 cups/236 ml chopped tomatoes, fresh or canned

6 cups/1.4 liters beef or chicken stock

8 medium red potatoes, peeled or unpeeled, cubed into 1-inch/2.5-cm pieces

4 medium carrots, peeled and cut into 1-inch/2.5-cm pieces on a diagonal

4 celery sticks, cut into 1-inch/2.5-cm pieces on a diagonal

1 cup/150 grams frozen peas

Chopped cilantro, optional garnish

Brown rice (see page 296), White rice (see page 298), or Quinoa (see page 294), optional

1. Rinse the stew meat and pat it dry with paper towels. Season it with plenty of salt and pepper.

2. In a large pot on medium to medium-high heat, add the fat of your choice and heat it until hot but never smoking. Add half of the stew meat and brown it on all sides.

3. Remove the meat to a medium bowl and add the other half of the stew meat to the pot, browning it on all sides. Remove the remaining meat from the pot to the bowl.

4. Add the onion (adding more fat, if needed) to the pot and sauté it for 5 minutes while stirring.

5. In a small separate bowl, combine the curry powder, garam masala, ginger, and garlic with enough water to make a paste. Add the paste to the onions in the pot and cook for 1 to 2 minutes, stirring constantly.

6. Add the tomatoes, stock, and stew meat to the pot and season generously with salt and pepper. Bring the stew to a simmer, reduce the heat, cover, and cook for 1½ hours.

7. Add the potatoes, carrots, and celery to the pot and cook the stew for another 30 minutes or until the vegetables are soft.

8. Right before serving, add the frozen peas to the pot and heat them through. Salt and pepper to taste and serve with cilantro to garnish, optional.

9. Serve the stew over rice or quinoa if desired.

GLUTEN-FREE
Grain-free
DAIRY-FREE

Chicken and Shrimp Gumbo

6–8 servings

Gumbo is most likely derived from the Bantu word for okra, as okra is one of the defining ingredients of gumbo. It's generally thickened using one of three methods: entirely with okra, with a roux made of flour and oil, or with filé, which is dried and ground sassafras leaves. My version uses okra and a roux.

Roux for gumbo is cooked for a long time. For the pictured gumbo, I cooked the roux for 25 minutes to reach a tan/cappuccino color. However, many gumbo enthusiasts cook their roux for 45–60 minutes or until the roux has reached a red/chocolate milk color. Roux cooked in this method produces a unique flavor profile, and the red/chocolate milk roux has an almost burnt flavor. I remain wary of the health implications of cooking flour in fat for such long periods of time, but many could not imagine gumbo without this distinction. If you would prefer to skip this step either for convenience or health concerns, know that many traditional gumbos were thickened entirely with okra. Follow the instructions for the okra-thickened version below. You can also add filé powder at the end of the cooking period to thicken it further if you can find it.

I find it unfortunate that most gumbos are made with inferior vegetable oils. Here, I use bacon grease (this is a great recipe to save your bacon grease for). Because high-quality shrimp is so expensive (avoid imported shrimp farmed in murky water), I've worked this recipe so that the shrimp can be left out for a chicken-only version, which is equally tasty.

8–10 slices thick-cut bacon, diced (enough to produce ¼ cup/60 ml of bacon grease)

¼ cup/25 grams white unbleached wheat or sweet rice flour

3 large celery sticks, diced

1 onion, peeled and finely chopped

1 green bell pepper, seeded, stemmed, and finely chopped

1 pound/450 grams okra, cut into ½-inch/1-2-cm pieces

3 garlic cloves, peeled and finely minced by hand or in a garlic press

1 pound/450 grams skinless, boneless chicken breasts or thighs, chopped into ½-inch/1.2-cm pieces

3 cups/710 ml chicken stock

1 teaspoon paprika

¾ teaspoon dried (not ground) thyme

½ teaspoon dried oregano

¼–¾ teaspoon cayenne pepper (depending on how spicy you want it)

1 teaspoon black pepper

½ pound/226 grams shrimp, deveined and peeled

GLUTEN-FREE
DAIRY-FREE

1. In a large pot, cook the diced bacon over medium heat, stirring as needed to prevent burning. When the bacon is crisp and browned, remove it with a slotted spoon and set aside.

2. Pour the bacon grease out of the pot and reserve it. Cool the pot and clean it well. Roux requires a clean pot. (You can also use ¼ cup saved bacon grease rather than the grease from the pot.)

3. Add the bacon grease and flour into the clean pot and return it to the stove over medium-low heat. Constantly stir the roux for 20–30 minutes, or until the roux reaches a dark tan. (See note above about roux color options.)

4. Add the vegetables to the pot and sprinkle them with salt. Cook the mixture over medium-heat, stirring as needed, for another 20 minutes This not only cooks the vegetables, but it also de-slimes the okra, releasing it to thicken the gumbo.

5. Add the chicken, chicken stock, paprika, thyme, oregano, cayenne pepper, black pepper, and reserved bacon to the pot. Bring the mixture to a simmer, turn the heat to low, and cook for 10 minutes.

6. Add the shrimp to the pot and continue cooking until the shrimp is just cooked through.

7. Salt and pepper to taste. Serve the gumbo over white rice (see page 296) or brown rice (see page 294).

Okra-Thickened Gumbo

Increase the okra to 1½ pounds/680 grams. Heat the bacon grease in a large pot over medium heat. Add all of the vegetables to the pot and sprinkle them with salt. Sauté for 20 minutes or until the vegetables are well cooked, the okra starts to break down, and the okra has given off much of the "slime" that it contains. Continue the recipe from Step 5.

Caramelized Onion and Potato Soup

6 servings

This soup makes a great base for all of the toppings you would typically put on a baked potato like sour cream, green onions, red onions, shredded cheddar cheese, crispy bacon bits, and even chili. Make the potato base and put on whatever toppings you want. The secret to this soup is getting the onions sweet by cooking them long enough.

2 tablespoons fat of your choice (see page 23)

4 cups/520 grams thinly sliced yellow or sweet onions

½ cup/120 ml dry white wine

3 pounds/1.3 kilograms potatoes, peeled and diced

1 teaspoon dried (not ground) thyme

2 bay leaves

6 cups/1.4 liters chicken or vegetable stock of choice

TOPPING CHOICES

Grated cheddar cheese

Sour cream

Bacon bits

Green onions

Chili

1. In a large pot, heat the fat of your choice over low to medium-low heat. Add the onions and sprinkle them generously with salt.

2. Slowly cook the onions, stirring to prevent premature browning, until they are limp, soft, and turning a light brown (25–30 minutes). They will have dramatically decreased in size and will be sweet to taste.

3. Add the wine to the pot and cook for 3 minutes.

4. Add the potatoes, thyme, bay leaves, and stock to the pot. Sprinkle generously with salt and pepper.

5. Bring the soup to a boil over high heat, turn the heat to low, cover, and cook until the potatoes are fork tender.

6. You can leave the soup chunky or purée part or all of the soup using an immersion blender or in batches in a blender or food processor. You can also mash some of the potatoes with a potato masher right in the pot to thicken the soup slightly.

7. Return the soup to the pot and reheat, adding more salt and pepper to taste. Thin the soup with extra broth, if needed.

8. Serve with the toppings of your choice.

Vegetarian-Friendly
GLUTEN-FREE
Grain-free
DAIRY-FREE
Budget-Friendly

Roasted Tomato and Bread Soup

8 servings

194

I could eat this soup every week. Oddly enough, it reminds me of a very pure, non-greasy pizza. I love that you can start with subpar tomatoes and end up with an incredibly flavorful soup through the roasting process.

A traditional version omits the roasting step, but tomatoes are only superior for a couple of months, if that, in Oregon. By roasting the tomatoes, you will bring out all of their sweetness and deepen their flavor. It isn't hard to do; it just takes a little time. I use Roma tomatoes in this recipe. They're cheaper than most varieties and great tasting.

If you don't like bread-thickened soups like this one, check out the Simple Cream of Tomato Soup on page 142.

2 pounds/900 grams Roma tomatoes, stemmed

4 tablespoons olive oil (traditional) or fat of your choice (see page 23), divided

1 large/2 small yellow onions, peeled and chopped

3 cloves garlic, peeled and finely minced by hand or in a garlic press

6 cups/1.4 liters chicken stock

1½ teaspoons Italian seasoning

2 tablespoons tomato paste

4 1-inch/2.5-cm slices crusty, artisan-style bread, cubed

Parmesan cheese, shredded for garnish (optional)

1. Preheat the oven to 350F/176C.

2. Cut the stemmed tomatoes in half, lengthwise. De-seed them by gently squeezing the tomatoes over a bowl. You can also pull the seeds out with your fingers.

3. In a jellyroll pan, toss the tomatoes with 2 tablespoons of the olive oil or fat of your choice. Sprinkle with salt and pepper and spread the tomatoes out on the pan. Roast for 1½ to 2 hours in the middle of the oven or until the tomatoes start to brown on the edges.

4. In a large pot, heat 2 tablespoons of the olive oil or fat of your choice over medium heat. Add the onions and garlic to the pot and sprinkle them with salt. Sauté for 5 minutes or until the onions are soft.

5. Add the chicken stock, Italian seasoning, tomato paste, and roasted tomatoes to the pot. Bring the soup to a boil, turn the heat to low, cover, and simmer for 10 minutes.

6. Add the cubed bread to the pot and simmer the soup for another 10 minutes. If it becomes too thick, thin it with a little extra stock.

7. Salt and pepper to taste and serve garnished with shredded Parmesan cheese (if using).

Garam Masala Chickpea Stew

6 servings/8–10 servings over rice

This creamy stew centers on chickpeas, spinach, and the beautiful spice blend of garam masala. I find that my children especially appreciate its appearance in soups. I have always enjoyed coconut milk with garam masala, which is why I paired them together in this soup. If you like it spicy, add a couple of pinches of red chili flakes. Once the chickpeas are cooked, this is so simple to put together. If you want to simplify it even more, you can use four cups of canned chickpeas. The kombu strip adds minerals as the chickpeas cook and makes them more digestible. Serve this stew over rice, if desired, or eat it alone.

2 cups/1 pound/450 grams dried chickpeas

1 kombu strip (optional)

2 tablespoons fat of your choice (see page 23)

1 medium yellow onion, peeled and chopped

3 garlic cloves, peeled and finely minced by hand or in a garlic press

2 cups/235 ml liquid (the liquid leftover from cooking chickpeas, vegetable broth, or chicken stock)

1 (14-ounce/414-ml) can full-fat coconut milk

1 tablespoon finely grated fresh ginger

1 tablespoon Garam Masala Spice Mixture (see page 276)

1 head spinach, stemmed and well-washed or 4 cups/120 grams baby spinach

Unrefined salt and freshly ground pepper

1. In a large covered bowl, soak the chickpeas overnight in warm water. Throw away any chickpeas that float. Drain and rinse.

2. Transfer the chickpeas to a pot and cover them with water that reaches 2-inches above the chickpeas. Add the kombu strip (if using) and bring the chickpeas to a simmer; cook about 1 hour or until they are soft.

3. In a large separate pot, heat the fat of your choice over medium to medium-high heat. Add the onions and garlic and sprinkle them with salt. Sauté for 5–7 minutes or until the vegetables are soft, stirring as needed to prevent burning.

4. Drain the cooked chickpeas, saving 2 cups of the cooking liquid.

5. Add the liquid, coconut milk, cooked chickpeas, ginger, garam masala, and a generous sprinkle of salt to the pot with the onions and garlic. Bring to a boil, lower the heat to low, cover and simmer for 10 minutes.

6. Add the spinach to the stew and cook it until wilted.

7. Salt and pepper to taste. Serve alone or over rice.

Oxtail Stew with Red Wine

6 servings

This simple, yet elegant, recipe utilizes red wine to add a lot of body to a lovely stew. Oxtail is amazing and especially suited to stews. In this recipe, red wine deepens the color of the meat to a dark brown. Oxtail is a fairly fatty cut, so you can skim fat off the surface of the soup if you prefer it less fatty.

2 tablespoons fat of your choice (see page 23)

1 medium yellow onion, peeled and chopped

1 celery stick, finely chopped

1 carrot, peeled, ends cut off and finely chopped

3 garlic cloves, peeled and thinly sliced

2½ pounds/1.15 kilograms meaty oxtail (you want at least 1 large oxtail piece for each serving, so at least 6)

2 cups/470 ml dry red wine

2 cups/470 ml beef or chicken stock

1 teaspoon dried thyme

2 bay leaves

1 teaspoon unrefined salt (leave out if using store-bought stock)

4 medium red potatoes/6 small, cubed into 1-inch/1.2-cm pieces

4 carrots, peeled and sliced into ½-inch/1.2-cm pieces on a diagonal

Chopped parsley, basil, or herb of your choice for garnish (optional)

1. In a large pot, heat the fat of your choice over medium to medium-high heat. Add the onion, celery, carrot, and garlic and sauté them until soft (5–7 minutes), stirring as needed to prevent burning. Remove the vegetables from the pot and set aside in a bowl.

2. Add more fat, if needed, to have a light layer of fat on the bottom of the pot. Pat the oxtail dry with paper towels and season it with salt and pepper. Brown both sides of the oxtail in two batches in the pot, flipping once, and setting aside the first batch with the vegetables while the second batch browns.

3. Return the vegetables and oxtail to the pot and add the red wine, stock, thyme, bay leaves, and salt. Bring the stew to a boil, scraping any browned pits off the bottom of the pan with a wooden spoon. Turn the heat to low, cover, and simmer for 3 hours or until the oxtail is fork tender but not falling off the bone.

4. Add the potatoes and carrots to the pot and cook another 20–30 minutes or until the vegetables are fork tender. Salt to taste.

5. Serve one large oxtail with broth and vegetables per person. It looks especially nice in a shallow bowl. Garnish with fresh herbs (if using).

Scotch Broth

10–12 servings

This Scottish soup is not really what we now consider a broth, but rather a hearty soup meant to be eaten as a main dish. The ingredients can vary, but barley and lamb are its important, distinctive flavors. Split peas add variety and more protein. You can substitute leeks for the onions, if you like. I was pleased that a friend who doesn't normally enjoy lamb ended up having a second bowl! To make this soup a more frugal choice, just use one small lamb shank. While lamb is not the cheapest meat, this recipe makes a very large pot of soup out of it. And if you'd like to skip the soaking process, use pearled barley instead of hulled.

1 cup/185 grams hulled barley

1 cup/235ml warm filtered water

1 tablespoon raw apple cider vinegar, yogurt, kefir, or other live-culture addition

½ cup/100 grams split peas

Warm filtered water

2 tablespoons fat of your choice (see page 23)

2 small/1 large lamb shank

2 small/1 large yellow onions, peeled and chopped

2 medium carrots, peeled and thinly sliced

2 celery sticks, thinly sliced

3 garlic cloves, peeled and thinly sliced

1½ teaspoons dried (not ground) thyme

2 bay leaves

12 cups/2.8 liters filtered water, lamb stock, chicken stock, or combination of stock and water

1 bunch of kale, washed

Chopped fresh parsley for garnish (optional)

1. Place the barley in a small bowl with one cup/235ml of warm filtered water and one tablespoon of raw apple cider vinegar or live-culture addition. In a separate bowl, cover the split peas with plenty of warm water. Cover both bowls and leave in a warm room for 12–24 hours. After the time has passed, drain the barley and split peas and rinse them well.

2. In a large pot, heat the fat of your choice over medium to medium-high heat. Add the lamb shanks to the pot and brown on both sides, turning as needed. Remove the lamb and set aside.

3. Add the onions, carrots, celery, and garlic to the pot (adding more fat, if needed) and sauté for 5 minutes, stirring as needed to prevent burning.

4. Return the lamb to the pot and add the thyme, bay leaves, and water and/or lamb broth. Bring the soup to a boil, turn the heat to low, cover and simmer for 1½ to 2 hours or until the lamb shanks are very tender and the meat is easy to pull off the bone. Remove the lamb shanks and let them cool.

5. While the lamb is cooling, stem the kale (unless using lacinato kale) and chop it into bite-sized pieces. Add the kale to the pot and simmer for 7 minutes or until the kale is soft.

6. Shred the lamb and return it to the pot. Salt well, starting with 2 teaspoons, and add freshly ground pepper if desired. Garnish with chopped parsley (if using) and serve.

Turkey and Wild Rice Soup

8–10 servings

I love making turkey broth, but we roast a turkey only so often. This soup allows you to make a large pot of soup using whatever turkey pieces you can find at the store (like turkey wings, drumsticks, or thighs). It's especially frugal with turkey wings!

½ cup/90 grams each wild rice and long-grain brown rice (or 1 cup/180 grams wild rice blend)

1 tablespoon raw apple cider vinegar

1 cup/236 ml warm filtered water

2 tablespoons fat of your choice (see page 23)

1 large/2 small yellow onions, peeled and chopped

4 medium carrots, peeled and sliced into ½-inch/1.2-cm pieces

4 celery sticks, sliced into ½-inch/1.2-cm pieces

3 medium garlic cloves, peeled and minced by hand or in a garlic press

10 cups/2.3 liters water

2 pounds/.9 kilogram turkey wings, thighs, or drumsticks

½ teaspoon each rubbed sage, dried thyme (not ground), and oregano or marjoram (or ¾ teaspoon poultry seasoning)

2 teaspoons of unrefined salt (plus more to taste) and freshly ground pepper

2 cups/120 grams sliced mushrooms

1 cup/110 grams frozen peas

Minced parsley (optional)

1. In a small bowl, combine the rice, raw apple cider vinegar, and warm water. Cover and leave in a warm place 12–24 hours. After the time has passed, rinse the rice well through a fine sieve.

2. In a large pot, heat the fat of your choice over medium to medium-high heat. Add the onions, carrots, celery, and garlic and sprinkle them with salt. Sauté, stirring as needed to prevent browning, for about 5 minutes or until the vegetables are soft.

3. Add the 10 cups/2.3 liters of water, turkey pieces, herbs, and 2 teaspoons of salt to the pot. Bring the soup to a simmer and turn the heat to low. Skim off any foam, cover, and cook the soup for 1 hour or more. The longer you cook, the more water the rice will absorb and the thicker the soup will become. At one hour, the soup has more broth. At 3 hours, it's thick.

4. Remove the turkey pieces and place them in a bowl to cool until they can be handled.

5. Salt and pepper the soup to taste, add the mushrooms, and cook for another 10 minutes.

6. Meanwhile, remove the skin from the turkey pieces, shred the turkey meat, and reserve the bones for making into more stock. Return the turkey meat to the soup.

7. Add the frozen peas to the soup and cook until heated through.

8. Top the soup with minced parsley (if using) and serve.

GLUTEN-FREE
DAIRY-FREE
Budget-Friendly

British Beef Stew with Dumplings

6 servings

204

If we were going to stereotype stews, we'd say that this is a "manly stew" if ever there was one. However, I find that women like it just as much as men. Stout gives it a very unique flavor: a deep, dark, slightly bitter background that makes it more interesting than the typical stew. The dumplings are an added bonus. Just make sure you keep them small, as they're moist when cooked in small portions. I restrained myself and kept this soup simple so that the beef and stout flavors would come out clearly, but I have to admit that I can easily imagine adding some green peas near the end of the cooking time, too.

2 tablespoons fat of your choice (see page 23)

6–8 medium carrots, peeled and cut into ½-inch/1.2-cm slices on a diagonal

2 medium/1 large yellow onion, chopped

3 garlic cloves, peeled and finely minced by hand or in a garlic press

¼ cup/25 grams flour (any type will do, including white rice flour)

2 pounds/.9 gram cubed stew beef, patted dry with paper towels

2 cups/470 ml beef stock

2 cups/470 ml stout or other dark beer

2 teaspoons finely minced dried rosemary or 1 tablespoon finely minced fresh rosemary

1 teaspoon unrefined salt

1 recipe of Herbed Dumplings (see page 286)

Chopped parsley for garnish (optional)

1. In a large pot, heat the fat of your choice over medium to medium-high heat. Add the carrots, onions, and garlic and sprinkle them with a pinch or two of salt. Sauté the vegetables for 5 minutes or until the vegetables start to soften, stirring as needed to prevent burning or browning. Remove the vegetables to a plate and turn off the heat.

2. In a large bowl, add the flour and toss it with a generous sprinkle of salt and pepper. Add the pieces of stew beef and turn them in the flour to coat them.

3. In the same pot as before, heat more fat, if needed, to coat the bottom. Add half of the meat to the pot and spread it out in a single layer on the bottom of the pan. Brown all sides of the meat and remove it to a plate. Spread the second half of the meat in a single layer on the bottom of the pan and brown it on sides. Remove it to the plate.

4. Add the beef stock to the pot and scrape all of the browned bits off the bottom as it heats. Add the stout, rosemary, and cooked vegetables to the pot.

5. Return the meat to the pot and add the salt (omit if using store-bought broth). Bring the stew to a boil, turn the heat to low, cover, and simmer for 1½ to 2 hours or until the meat is very tender.

6. Salt and pepper the stew to taste.

7. Make the dumplings according to the directions on page 286.

8. Garnish with parsley (if using) and serve.

Spring Chicken Soup

6–8 servings

This soup is a celebration of springtime. Loaded with vegetables, including asparagus and watercress, it makes a flavorful broth while it cooks. For double the flavor and nutrition, you can use chicken broth instead of water. I like to slice the potatoes into thin circles for this soup. It makes a more delicate presentation than cubed potatoes.

2 tablespoons fat of your choice (see page 23)

1 large yellow onion, peeled and chopped

4 celery sticks, cut into 1-inch/2.5-cm pieces on a diagonal

4 carrots, peeled, cut in half lengthwise, and cut into 1-inch/2.5-cm pieces on a diagonal

3 garlic cloves, peeled and smashed

1½ pounds/680 grams chicken drumsticks

8 cups/1.9 liters filtered water or chicken stock

1½ teaspoons dried (not ground) thyme or several sprigs of fresh thyme

2 bay leaves

2 teaspoons unrefined salt (leave out if using store-bought stock instead of water)

2 large/3 medium russet potatoes, scrubbed and sliced into ⅛-inch/.30-cm rounds (omit or replace with a GAPS-friendly root vegetable such as celery root, if desired)

½–¾ pound/226–340 grams asparagus, woody parts of the stem cut off and discarded, and the rest cut into 2-inch/5-cm pieces

1 bunch watercress, the very ends of the stems cut off

1. In a large pot, heat the fat of your choice over medium to medium-high heat. Add the onions, celery, carrots, and garlic. Sprinkle them with salt and sauté them for 5 minutes, stirring as needed to prevent burning.

2. Add the chicken, water or chicken stock, thyme, bay leaves, and 2 teaspoons of salt to the pot (if you aren't using store-bought stock). Bring the soup to a boil and turn the heat to low. Cover and gently simmer for 1 to 1½ hours.

3. Remove the drumsticks from the pot and set them aside to cool.

4. Add the potatoes and asparagus to the pot and cook the soup for 7 minutes or until the potatoes are just tender.

5. Add the watercress to the pot and cook until it is just wilted (about 1 minute).

6. Remove the skin off of the chicken legs and shred the chicken meat. Add the shredded chicken to the soup, saving the bones for stock.

7. Salt and pepper the soup to taste and serve.

Leek and Potato Soup

6–8 servings

208

This simple soup is a winning combination of sweet leeks, filling potatoes, and rich butter. With so few ingredients, you might expect this soup to be bland, but the leeks really make this soup sing. As always, make sure that you wash the leeks well because they can be gritty. I prefer the soup chunky, but you can also purée part or all of the soup, if you like.

2 tablespoons of fat of your choice (see page 23)

2 large/4 medium leeks, thinly sliced (see page 33 for directions)

3 pounds/1.3 kilograms potatoes of your choice (Yukon golds are especially nice), peeled, if desired, and cut into large cubes

1½ teaspoons dried thyme or a couple sprigs of fresh thyme

2 bay leaves

6 cups/1.4 liters chicken or vegetable stock

¼ cup/60 grams butter, preferably pastured

1. In a large pot, heat the fat of your choice over medium to medium-high heat. Add the leeks and sprinkle them generously with salt. Sauté the leeks for 7–10 minutes or until the leeks soften.

2. Add the potatoes, thyme, bay leaves, and stock to the pot. Add another generous sprinkle of salt and bring the soup to a boil. Turn the heat to low and gently simmer for 20 minutes or until the potatoes are soft.

3. Add the butter and allow it to melt.

4. Salt and pepper to taste and serve.

Vegetarian-Friendly
GLUTEN-FREE
Grain-free
DAIRY-FREE

Pot-au-Feu

8 servings

This lovely family-style French beef stew has a long history, with its origins going far back in history. The basic concept of long-simmering beef, bones, and vegetables was a method well adapted to historical lifestyles and cooking methods. Every region has its own take on Pot-au-Feu, such as adding sausage or other cuts of meat. I think all variations would be delicious!

While we associate the word "stew" with chunky thick soups, this stew is eaten differently. After the meat and vegetables are done, they are removed from the broth and served separately, with the broth served on its own. Because you don't brown the vegetables or the meat while making this dish, the broth is especially mild. Use any leftover broth for other soups.

Try serving it with crusty bread and butter or steamed potatoes, which is also traditional. Potatoes were typically cooked separately, as the starch they would release into the broth was considered undesirable. A fun variation might be to cook some pasta in the broth after the vegetables and meat are removed—appealing to both adults and children.

The additional (but traditional) marrowbones, soup bones, or oxtail make the broth more nutritious, as well as rich and tasty. However, the recipe still works without them. The oxtails are especially nice as an additional meat item in the soup (serve alongside the roast, and people can individually cut the meat off the bone). The marrowbones can be served with crusty bread. Provide small knives for people to spread the marrow onto toast.

4–5 pounds/1.8–2.26 kilograms pot roast (such as rump roast, chuck roast, or top round)

1 pound/453 grams soup bones, oxtail, or marrow bones, optional

2 bay leaves

Several sprigs fresh thyme or 1½ teaspoons dried (not ground) thyme

1 garlic clove, peeled

12 cups/2.8 liters filtered water

1 yellow onion, peeled

4 whole cloves

2 medium leeks, washed, trimmed and cut into ½-inch/1.3-cm pieces (see page 33)

4 celery sticks, cut into 1-inch/2.5-cm pieces

4 carrots, peeled and cut into 2-inch/5-cm pieces

4 turnips, peeled and cut into eighths

Half large bunch Italian parsley, stemmed and chopped

Optional serving suggestions

Dijon-style mustard or brown mustard

Gherkins

Steamed potatoes

Crusty bread

GLUTEN-FREE
GAPS-friendly
DAIRY-FREE

1. In a large pot, add the pot roast; soup bones, oxtail, or marrow bones (if using); bay leaves; thyme; garlic; and water. Stick the four cloves into the onion and add it to the pot. Bring the soup to a boil over high heat.

2. Turn the heat to low, cover and simmer for 2–4 hours. Skim any foam that rises. The meat should be fork tender and easily cut into pieces when done.

3. A half hour before serving, add the leeks, celery, carrots, and turnips to the pot. Return the soup to a low simmer for 30 minutes or until the vegetables are soft.

4. Remove the onion from the pot if it hasn't completely fallen apart, and the pot roast, bones/oxtail, and vegetables, and place them on a serving platter. Put the serving platter in a warm oven.

5. Taste the broth. If it is weak, bring it to a boil and reduce the liquid to produce a richer broth.

6. Salt and pepper the broth generously to taste.

7. Right before serving, sprinkle the broth and the meat/vegetable serving platter generously with parsley.

8. The broth can be served as a first course and the meat and vegetables as a second, but we like to serve it all together. The meat is especially delicious when dipped into a good mustard. (If you have any leftover broth, use it in other recipes.)

Chicken and Dumplings

4–6 servings

This version of chicken and dumplings is plump with vegetables and soft dumplings. When I was developing this recipe, we liked it so much, we ate it with pleasure several days in a row. I have thickened it slightly, but that is completely optional.

2 tablespoons fat of your choice (see page 23)

6 medium carrots, peeled and diced or thinly sliced

4 celery sticks, thinly sliced or diced

1 medium yellow onion, peeled and chopped

3 garlic cloves, peeled and finely minced by hand or in a garlic press

2 tablespoons white unbleached wheat or white rice flour

6 cups/1.4 liters chicken stock

1 teaspoon dried (not ground) thyme

1½ teaspoons dried basil

¼ teaspoon turmeric (optional)

¾ pound/340 grams skinless, boneless chicken breasts or thighs, diced

1 Herbed Dumpling recipe (start the soaking process the night before; see page 286)

1 cup/110 grams frozen peas

Fresh, minced herbs for garnish (optional)

1. In a large pot, heat the fat of your choice over medium to medium-high heat. Add the carrots, celery, onion, and garlic to the pot and sprinkle generously with salt. Sauté, stirring as needed, until the vegetables soften (about 7 minutes).

2. Sprinkle the flour into pot, stir, and cook it for 1 minute more.

3. Add the stock, thyme, basil, turmeric (if using), and chicken. Bring the soup to a low simmer and cook for 5–7 minutes or until the chicken is cooked through. Salt and pepper to taste.

4. Bring the soup to a rapid boil. Add the dumplings in by tablespoons as per the dumpling recipe directions. Cover and keep at a rumbling simmer for 8 minutes or until the ingredients are cooked through.

5. Gently add the frozen peas, scooting them by the dumplings into the hot broth, to heat them through.

6. Top the soup with the fresh herbs (if using) and serve.

Italian Vegetable and Sausage Soup

6–8 servings

My mother-in-law often made a soup similar to this one a lot and it was a favorite of us all. There is something so refreshing and filling about it. I love the long green beans, zucchini, and sausage. Use the ½ pound/226 grams of sausage for a lighter soup to serve as a first course. Serve with buttered bread for a heartier main dish soup.

2 tablespoons fat of your choice (see page 23)

1 large/2 small yellow onions, peeled and chopped

1 red bell pepper, stemmed, seeded, and chopped (optional)

3–6 garlic cloves, peeled and finely minced by hand or in a garlic press

6 cups/1.4 liters chicken stock

2 teaspoons Italian herbs (you can use your own combination of herbs such as oregano, basil, thyme, marjoram, rosemary, and parsley, if desired)

2 cups/470 ml fresh or canned diced tomatoes

1 teaspoon unrefined salt (omit if using store-bought stock)

½–1 pound/226–450 grams bulk Italian sausage

2 medium/4 small thinly sliced zucchini squash

¾ pound/340 grams green beans, stemmed, snapped in half or left long

½ bunch parsley, diced

1. In a large pot, heat the fat of your choice over medium to medium-high heat. Add the onions, red bell pepper (if using), and garlic cloves. Sprinkle generously with salt and sauté, stirring as needed to prevent browning, until the vegetables are soft.

2. Add the chicken stock, herbs, and tomatoes to the pot.

3. Add the salt (omit if using store-bought stock).

4. If you're using a very lean sausage, add it right in the pot to cook with the vegetables. Otherwise, cook the sausage in a large saucepan while the vegetables cook, removing any grease with a spoon before adding the sausage to the soup.

5. Add the zucchini squash and green beans to the pot and bring the soup to a simmer. Cook for 7 minutes or until the vegetables are cooked, as well as the sausage if you are cooking it in the soup.

6. Salt and pepper the soup to taste, top it with the parsley, and serve.

Lamb Stew

8 servings

*L*amb is a special treat in our household. Since lamb stew meat is so expensive, we don't have it as often as we'd like, but this stew uses a smaller amount of meat, which helps us to enjoy it more often. To give it a really lovely lamb-y flavor, use lamb stock. Thankfully, I'm able to buy lamb bones cheaply to make lamb stock. If you can't find lamb bones, though, chicken stock works well. It's delectable by itself or served over mashed potatoes, rice, or quinoa.

1½ pounds/680 grams lamb stew meat, cut into 1½-inch/3.8-cm pieces

¼ cup/25 grams flour (unbleached white, wheat, rice, sprouted, or arrowroot flour)

2 tablespoons fat of your choice (see page 23)

1 large yellow onion, peeled and finely chopped

1 carrot, peeled and diced

1 celery stick, diced

3 garlic cloves, peeled and thinly sliced

1 cup/236 ml white wine

4 cups/.9 liter lamb or chicken stock

1½ teaspoons dried (not ground) oregano or thyme

2 bay leaves

6 carrots, peeled and sliced into ½-inch/1.2-cm pieces on a diagonal

4 celery sticks, sliced into ½-inch/1.2-cm on a diagonal

6 medium potatoes, diced into 1- to 1½-inch/2.5-3.8-cm pieces

2 tablespoons soft butter mixed well with 2 tablespoons of flour (optional—for a thicker soup)

1 cup/110 grams frozen peas

1. Dry the lamb meat with paper towels and set aside.

2. In a large bowl, mix the flour with a generous sprinkle of salt and pepper. Toss the lamb meat in the bowl to coat with the flour.

3. In a large pot, heat the fat of your choice over medium to medium-high heat. Add the onion, garlic and diced carrot, and celery to the pot. Sprinkle the ingredients with salt and sauté, stirring as needed to prevent burning, until the vegetables are soft.

4. Remove the vegetables from the pot and set aside.

5. Add more fat to the pot, if needed, for a total of 2 tablespoons. Add half of the lamb meat and brown it on all sides. Remove the meat and set it aside. Add the remaining lamb meat to the pot and brown it on all sides. Leave this half of the lamb in the pot.

6. Add the wine to the pot and as it simmers scrape any browned bits off the bottom of the pan.

7. Add the stock, oregano, thyme, bay leaves, the remaining lamb, and the cooked vegetables to the pot. Bring the stew to a boil, turn the heat to low, cover, and simmer for 1½ hours.

8. Add the uncooked vegetables (6 carrots, 4 celery sticks, and potatoes) and bring the stew to a simmer. Cook for another 30 minutes.

9. If the stew is too thin, add the butter and flour mixture and simmer it for several minutes until it is thicker.

10. Add the peas to the pot and remove the bay leaves.

11. Salt and pepper the stew to taste and serve it when the peas are heated through.

Jamaican Oxtail Soup

10–12 servings

This stew stretches out the wonderful oxtail cut with plenty of white beans (about 6 cups). Lima beans were traditionally used, but I enjoy the smaller white beans in this recipe. You can use canned (well-rinsed) beans, but I recommend homemade. The allspice is an important, traditional part of the soup, as is the spice from a hot pepper.

3 cups/1½ pounds/680 grams dried small white beans (Use navy beans for GAPS-friendly)

2 tablespoons fat of your choice (see page 23)

1 large yellow onion, peeled and chopped

3 large garlic cloves, peeled and thinly sliced

2 pounds/900 grams oxtail

1 cup/236 ml tomato sauce or ¼ cup/60 ml tomato paste

¾ teaspoon allspice

1 teaspoon dried thyme

2 bay leaves

1 jalapeño or other hot pepper, stemmed and finely chopped (seed if you want less heat; use two hot peppers for extra spiciness; protect your hands with gloves)

2 tablespoons coconut sugar, whole cane sugar, or other sweetener (use honey for GAPS-friendly)

6 cups/1.4 liters beef or chicken stock

1 teaspoon unrefined salt

1. Soak the white beans in plenty of warm water for 12–24 hours. Drain and rinse well.

2. In a large separate pot, heat the fat of your choice over medium to medium-high heat. Add the onion and garlic and sprinkle them with salt. Sauté for 5–7 minutes until soft, stirring to prevent burning, Remove the onion and garlic from the pot and set them aside in a bowl.

3. Meanwhile, pat the oxtail dry with paper towels and season it with salt and pepper.

4. Add more fat to the pot if needed and place the oxtail at the bottom in a thin layer. Brown both sides of the meat in two batches (setting aside the first batch alongside the onion and garlic).

5. Add the tomato sauce or paste to the hot pan and sizzle it for 30 seconds.

6. Add the meat, onion and garlic, allspice, thyme, bay leaves, pepper, sugar, stock, and salt to the pot. Bring the soup to a boil, turn the heat to low, cover, and simmer for about 3 hours or until the oxtail is fork-tender.

7. Meanwhile, cook the soaked and rinsed white beans in a separate pot. Cover them with plenty of water (at least 2-inches above the surface of the beans), bring to a boil, and turn the heat to low. Simmer for 45 minutes or until the beans are tender. Drain the water from the pot.

8. When the oxtail is tender and easy to pull off the bone, remove it from the pot with tongs, set it aside to cool. Remove the bay leaves from the soup as well. If you don't want the soup to be very fatty, you can skim some or all of the fat from the surface.

GLUTEN-FREE
Grain-free
GAPS-friendly
DAIRY-FREE

9. Add the beans to the stew and heat them through again.

10. Shred the meat off of the oxtail and add it back to the pot (discarding any fatty parts). To de-fat the broth and to further meld flavors, refrigerate at this point and skim off any fat from the surface of the soup once chilled. Reheat.

11. Salt and pepper the soup to taste and serve over rice.

Seafood Soups

Seafood soups are something special with their briny flavor. Not only are they delicious but most seafood is very healthy too. Dr. Weston A. Price considered seafood an especially nourishing food, and for good reason. Most of us are deficient in omega-3 fatty acids, and salmon, black cod, and certain other seafood items are high in it. Mussels, oysters, and clams are high in B vitamins, and seafood in general is an excellent source of protein.

However, it's important to buy high-quality seafood. I avoid all farmed salmon, for example, as it contains low amounts of omega-3 fatty acids and can be high in toxins. Plus, farmed salmon is prone to infections and is often given high amounts of antibiotics, not to mention the fact that many of the fisheries pollute the surrounding environment. I buy wild Alaskan salmon or wild salmon from Washington, California, or Oregon. I buy farmed mussels and clams that are farmed in their natural environment (though I now avoid local oysters because I found out that their farming area is often sprayed with toxic herbicides to control algae growth).

My goal is to consume eco-safe seafood that is low in mercury and other toxins and high in nutrients. Wild salmon, black cod, sardines, and other small fish fit the bill, as do many shellfish. Large fish are higher in mercury and other toxins, so best avoided. Wild Alaskan halibut is a great fish that has a good nutrient profile, but since it's a larger fish, it does contain a moderate mercury level. For that reason, it's best not to eat it often, especially when pregnant or when feeding young children.

Bay shrimp are generally net caught and wild, and the smaller species are usually cleaner than the large ones. So, go small! Don't buy farmed shrimp, especially tiger prawns; they're grown in disreputable conditions and are typically laced with toxins.

When buying fresh seafood, get the freshest possible and cook it the same night. Otherwise, it will become more and more "fishy" in taste.

Other soups with seafood:

The Proper Care of Manila Clams and Mussels

Buying

The clams should smell appealing and the shell should be intact. A good fish market will handpick the clams for you to make sure that there are no dead clams in them. Ask how long the clams have been in the store and try to shop when a new shipment has arrived. Manila clams are readily available in my area, however my recipes could be easily adapted to what is available to you.

Storing

Never keep clams or mussels in a sealed bag or container, as you could suffocate and kill them. The best storing solution is to lay them in a wide and shallow dish like a pie pan and cover them with a damp towel. They will generally stay fresh for a couple of days like this, but the longer you keep them, the greater the chance that they will die. They also taste best when they're fresher.

Cleaning

Rinse them with several washes of water. When the water hits the clams, the live ones will shut, which also helps you see if any have died. Throw away any that won't close when gently pressed to a closing position. If they are very dirty, you can scrub them with a potato brush. To de-sand them, place them in a bowlful of cool water with one tablespoon of flour or cornmeal. Leave them in the water for 20 minutes, remove them from the water, and rinse right before cooking.

For Mussels

Follow the same instructions as for the clams. The one extra step involves removing the "beard" of the mussel, also known as the byssal thread. After cleaning the mussels and de-sanding them, remove the "beard" right before cooking. Hold the mussel in one hand, cover the other hand with a dry towel, grasp the beard, and give it a sharp yank toward the hinge end of the mussel. Discard the beard.

Lemongrass Clam Chowder

6–8 main-dish servings

This rich and creamy clam chowder is a delight and a wonderful way to get nutrient- dense clams into your diet. Instead of having a long list of authentic Thai ingredients in this recipe, forcing you to search local Asian markets, I've kept things pretty simple. The only hard-to-find ingredient is lemongrass, which is becoming more and more available at regular supermarkets. It's the high point of the soup, although the bacon, clams, ginger, and coconut milk help, too. I love how pretty Manila clamshells are in soup. My sister-in-law adds a large can of clams in place of the fresh clams, and that also works fine.

4 slices of bacon, diced

1 large yellow onion, peeled and chopped

1 large red bell pepper, washed, seeded, and chopped

3 medium garlic cloves, peeled and sliced into thin slices

1 tablespoon grated fresh ginger

6 medium potatoes, peeled and cubed

6 cups/1.4 liters chicken or fish stock

Pinch of red pepper flakes

1 stalk of lemongrass, washed thoroughly

1 (14-ounce/414 ml) can full-fat coconut milk

1–2 pounds/450–900 grams fresh, live Manila clams

¼ cup/60 ml freshly squeezed lime juice

¼ bunch of cilantro (optional)

1. In a large pot, fry the bacon over medium heat until crisp, stirring to brown evenly. Remove the bacon from the pot with a slotted spoon and cool.

2. Pour off most of the bacon grease, leaving about 2 tablespoons in the pot. (I always save my bacon grease to use in other recipes.)

3. Add the onion and red bell pepper to the pot and sauté over medium-high heat until the onion starts to soften. Add the garlic and ginger to the pot and sauté for about 1 minute, not allowing the garlic to brown.

4. Add the potatoes, stock, crumbled bacon, red pepper flakes, and a generous sprinkle of salt to the pot. Cut the ends off of the lemongrass and peel off the tough outer layers. Cut the lemongrass in half and place it in the soup as well.

5. Bring the soup to a boil and turn the heat to low. Cover and cook for 15 minutes or until the potatoes are soft.

6. Add the coconut milk to the pot and return the soup to a simmer.

7. Remove any open or cracked clams. Add the clams to the pot, cooking until all of the clams are open (about 3-5 minutes). Remove any that didn't open.

8. Fish the lemongrass out of the pot and add the lime juice and cilantro (if using) and serve extra cilantro on the side.

9. Salt and pepper the soup to taste and serve.

Simple White Fish and Rice Soup

6–8 servings

Like a chicken and rice soup but with fish, this recipe is simple and kid-friendly. Since fresh seafood is such a tasty and nutritious food, it's nice to have less complicated recipes for it. For an extra punch of flavor, garnish the soup with fresh herbs, such as basil, or add Pesto (see page 274). Salmon can be substituted for the white fish, too.

2 tablespoons fat of your choice (see page 23)

2 small/1 large yellow onions, peeled and chopped

4 celery sticks, diced or thinly sliced

3 garlic cloves, peeled and finely minced by hand or in a garlic press

½ cup/120 ml dry white wine

¾ cup/135 grams long grain white rice*

8 cups/1.9 liters Rich Fish Stock (see page 58), Simple Fish Stock (see page 56), or Basic Chicken Stock (see page 44)

1 teaspoon dried (not ground) thyme

1 teaspoon dried basil

¾–1 pound/340–450 grams white fish, such as halibut or cod, all bones and skin removed, diced

1 cup/110 grams frozen peas

Fresh parsley, basil, or thyme, minced (optional)

1. In a large pot, heat the fat of your choice over medium to medium-high heat. Sauté the onions, celery, and garlic in the pot with a sprinkle of salt for 5 minutes or until the vegetables start to soften. Stir to prevent burning.

2. Add the white wine, rice, stock, thyme, and basil to the pot, with another generous sprinkle of salt and bring the soup to a simmer. Turn the heat to low, cover, and simmer for 20 minutes.

3. Add the fish to the pot and gently simmer for 5–7 minutes or until the fish is cooked through.

4. Add the frozen peas to the pot and heat until cooked through. Salt and pepper to taste, top the soup with chopped fresh parsley or herb of your choice (if using), and serve.

*Brown Rice Version

Combine ¾ cup/160 grams of brown rice with 1 cup/236 ml of warm water and 1 tablespoon of raw apple cider vinegar, yogurt, kefir, buttermilk, whey, or other live-culture addition in a bowl and cover. Leave the mixture in a warm place for 12–24 hours. After the time has passed, rinse the rice well through a fine sieve and drain. Cook the rice for 45 minutes in Step 2 instead of 20 minutes.

Mussels in Tomato Garlic Broth

4 first-course servings or 2 hearty main dishes

228

I love mussels for a variety of reasons. They are very nutritious, delicious, and easy to prepare. In this case, they are steamed in a simple tomato garlic broth, which becomes salty and briny from the mussels. The broth is perfect to sop up with crusty bread. One recipe tester added a pinch of red pepper flakes and used frozen mussels with success. If you use frozen mussels, just follow the cooking time on the package.

2 pounds/.9 kilogram mussels, prepared (see page 222)

2 tablespoons olive oil

2 medium/1 large tomatoes

3 garlic cloves, peeled and finely minced

½ cup/120 ml dry white wine

1 cup/236 ml stock of your choice or water

Handful of fresh basil, stemmed, rolled into a cigar shape, and cut into thin shreds, or torn into small pieces

1. Prepare the mussels ahead of time according to the instructions on page 222.

2. In a large pot or saucepan with a lid, heat the olive oil over medium heat until hot but never smoking. Sauté the tomatoes and garlic in the oil for 3 minutes.

3. Add the wine to the pot and cook for 5 minutes or until the tomatoes are falling apart.

4. Add the stock or water to the pot and bring the soup to a boil.

5. Add the mussels to the pot and cover it. Turn the heat to low and steam the mussels until all of them are open (5–8 minutes depending on the size of the mussels). The mussels should never be overcooked or they will become tough and chewy.

6. Remove any mussels that didn't open and throw them away.

7. Sprinkle the broth with fresh basil and serve with crusty bread and a big bowl for discarding the empty shells.

Clam Version

Substitute small Manila clams for the mussels and reduce the cooking time in Step 4 to 3–5 minutes.

White Fish Soup with Fennel, Green Beans, and Tomatoes

6–8 servings

230

This soup is simple but fancy. I use the fronds (the top) of a stalk of fennel to make a light fennel broth. This forms the base for a light fish and vegetable soup that's lovely with a salad on a hot day.

1 small fennel with fronds, thinly sliced, fronds reserved for the broth

6 cups/1.4 liters water

2 tablespoons fat of your choice (see page 23)

2 medium leeks, thinly sliced (see page 33)

4 medium/large tomatoes

3 cloves garlic, peeled and finely minced by hand or in a garlic press

1 tablespoon tomato paste

½ cup/120 ml dry white wine

1½ teaspoons salt

1 pound/450 grams green beans

1 pound/450 grams skinless, boned white fish (I suggest Alaskan halibut, cod, or black cod), cut into ½-inch/1.2-cm pieces

Chopped basil or Delicious Pesto (see page 274) for garnish (optional)

1. To make the fennel broth, place the fronds in a medium pot and add the water. Bring to a boil and turn the heat to low. Cover and simmer for 20 minutes. Strain and set the broth aside.

2. In a large pot, heat the fat of your choice over medium to medium-high heat. Add the sliced leeks and sliced fennel to the pot and sprinkle with salt. Sauté for 5 minutes or until the vegetables are soft. Add the tomatoes and garlic to the pot and cook for another 5 minutes or until the tomatoes become soft and start to fall apart.

3. Push the vegetables away from the middle of the pot, add the tomato paste, and let it sizzle for 30 seconds.

4. Add the white wine and fennel broth to the pot. Add 1½ teaspoons of salt to the pot and bring the soup to a boil.

5. Add green beans to the pot and simmer for 2 minutes.

6. Add the fish to the pot and simmer for another 5 minutes or until the green beans are tender and the fish is cooked through.

7. Salt and pepper the soup to taste, garnish with chopped basil or pesto, if desired, and serve.

Poor Man's Bouillabaisse

6–8 servings

Bouillabaisse is a traditional Provençal fish stew that contains at least three kinds of fish and other seafood such as shellfish, sea urchins, crabs, or octopus. Rather than try to recreate a Marseille experience here in the States, I've chosen to break a few rules and make a more budget-friendly stew with the fresh seafood available to me. Thankfully, this recipe is actually quite simple to prepare! We are left with a flavorful broth lightly brightened with citrus, saffron, and wine; herbed with parsley and fresh thyme; and further flavored with sweet leeks and fresh fennel. While certainly much cheaper than many versions, because of the saffron and seafood, this is still a special occasion soup for us, but one that we greatly enjoy. For best flavor, buy the greatest variety of seafood you can.

½–¾ pound/226–340 grams small Manila clams, prepared (see page 222)

½–¾ pound/226–340 grams mussels, prepared (see page 222)

8 cups/1.9 liters fish stock of your choice (see pages 56-60)

1 small fennel, thinly sliced (keep the fronds—the top part of the fennel)

1 medium leek, thinly sliced (see page 33)

2 garlic cloves, peeled and thinly sliced

Zest from ½ of one large orange

Juice from one orange

½ cup/120 ml dry white wine

Pinch of saffron

6–8 sprigs fresh thyme

2 bay leaves

2 teaspoons salt

Ground black pepper

1 pound/450 grams deboned and skinned white fish, such as halibut, rockfish, or black cod (you can also use several types of white fish, for even more flavor), chopped into 1-inch/2.5-cm pieces

¼ cup/10 grams chopped parsley

Fresh lemon juice (optional)

Sauce Rouille (see opposite page)

Fresh thyme for garnish

1. Prepare the clams and mussels according to the instructions on page 222.

2. In a large pot, heat the fish stock with the thinly sliced fennel, reserved fennel fronds, leeks, garlic, orange zest, orange juice, wine, saffron, thyme, bay leaves, and salt. Add a generous amount of black pepper to taste. Simmer for 10 minutes on low heat. Remove the fennel fronds.

3. Add the white fish and mussels to the pot and cook for 5 minutes.

4. Add the clams and parsley to the pot and cook for 3–5 minutes more or until the clams have opened. Discard any clams or mussels that didn't open.

5. Season to taste with salt, pepper, and/or lemon juice.

6. Serve the soup over a slice of bread or with bread to dip into the broth. Garnish with a spoonful of Sauce Rouille and fresh thyme.

DAIRY-FREE

Sauce Rouille

About 1 cup

*T*his version of rouille is like a sweet, eggless mayo spiked with garlic and cayenne. It makes a flavorful addition to a soup. The roasted bell pepper adds sweetness to the sauce that melds well with the sweetness of the fennel and leeks in the broth. You can make this sauce as spicy or as mild as you like by varying the cayenne.

1 slice white bread or bread of your choice, crust cut off

1 red bell pepper, roasted, skinned, and seeded

¼–½ teaspoon cayenne pepper (¼ teaspoon for a mild sauce)

½ teaspoon salt

2 garlic cloves, peeled and finely chopped

2 tablespoons lemon juice

½ cup/120 ml extra-virgin olive oil

Water or fish stock to thin the sauce, if needed

1. In a food processor, add the bread and pulse until it reaches a fine breadcrumb consistency.

2. Add the red bell pepper, cayenne pepper, salt, garlic, and lemon juice to the food processor. Blend until smooth.

3. Add the oil and pulse until just combined with the sauce. If the rouille is too thick, thin it with water or fish stock.

Creamy Salmon Chowder

6–8 servings

This creamy soup is a delight and a delicious way to enjoy salmon. If you like a thinner chowder, leave out the flour. I also enjoy the bacon in this recipe, but you could certainly substitute butter or another fat for the bacon grease. I highly recommend that you allow this soup to rest for a couple of hours or overnight to allow the flavors to meld fully.

6 slices bacon

1 large/2 small yellow onions, peeled and chopped

3 garlic cloves, peeled and finely minced by hand or in a garlic press

4 celery sticks, diced

⅓ cup/30 grams unbleached white, white rice, sprouted flour, or arrowroot

4–5 medium red or Yukon potatoes, diced into ½-inch/1.2-cm cubes, peeled if desired (about 4 cups)

4 cups/.9 liter fish or chicken stock

1 teaspoon unrefined salt

Several sprigs fresh thyme or 1 teaspoon dried thyme (not ground)

2 bay leaves

1–1½ pounds/450–680 grams skinless, boneless wild salmon, cut into ½-inch/1.2-cm cubes

2 cups/470 ml whole milk or Homemade Almond Milk (see page 292)

Fresh parsley or basil for garnish (optional)

1. In a large pot, fry the bacon over medium heat until crisp. Remove the bacon from the pot and cool it. When cool, crumble it and set aside. Remove the extra bacon grease from the pot except for two tablespoons of grease.

2. Add the onions, garlic, and celery sticks to the pot and sauté over medium to medium-high heat until soft (5–7 minutes), stirring as needed to prevent burning.

3. Add the flour to the pot and stir until it is well mixed with the vegetables.

4. Add the potatoes, stock, 1 teaspoon of salt (leave out if using store-bought stock), thyme, bay leaves, and crumbled bacon into the chowder. Bring the soup to a simmer and turn the heat to low. Simmer for 15 minutes or until the potatoes are just soft.

5. Add the salmon and milk to the pot and return it to a very low simmer for 5 minutes or until the salmon is cooked and soft.

6. Remove the bay leaves, add salt and pepper to taste, garnish the chowder with the parsley or basil (if using), and serve.

Variation

Adding one diced red pepper in Step 2 and/ or adding 1 cup of fresh corn cut of the cob, or frozen, is also delicious!

Clams in a Spicy Tomato Broth with Bacon

4 first-course servings or 2 main-dish servings

This is another simple way to prepare clams. They are simmered in a spicy, bacon-y broth that is perfect for sopping up with a piece of bread. Place a bowl alongside the clams for people to place their empty shells. If you use larger clams, you'll just need to cook longer. You can use frozen clams, just follow the package instructions for cooking time.

2 pounds/450 grams small Manila clams, prepared (see page 222)

6 slices bacon

5 medium garlic cloves, peeled and thinly sliced

6 Roma tomatoes, chopped

½ cup/120 ml dry white wine

1 teaspoon dried oregano

½–1 teaspoon chipotle pepper flakes (or regular pepper flakes)

1 cup/236 ml water or stock of your choice

Fresh cilantro, chopped (optional)

1. Prepare the clams ahead of time according to the instructions on page 222.

2. In a large pot or saucepan with a lid, cook the bacon over medium heat until crispy and browned, flipping as needed to cook evenly. Remove the bacon and set it aside to cool.

3. Add the garlic and tomatoes to the pot and sauté for 7 minutes or until the tomatoes are broken down.

4. Add the white wine, oregano, and pepper flakes to the pot and cook for 2–3 minutes more to continue to break down the tomatoes.

5. Add the water or stock to the pot and bring to a boil.

6. Add the clams to the pot and cover it. Turn the heat to low and keep the soup at a simmer. Cook until the clams are all open (5 minutes or less). Remove any clams that didn't open.

7. Salt the broth to taste if needed. Crumble the bacon over the soup and add a handful of chopped cilantro for garnish if desired.

Mussel Version

Substitute mussels for the clams. Cook for 5–8 minutes, depending on the size of the mussels.

GLUTEN-FREE
Grain-free
GAPS-friendly
DAIRY-FREE

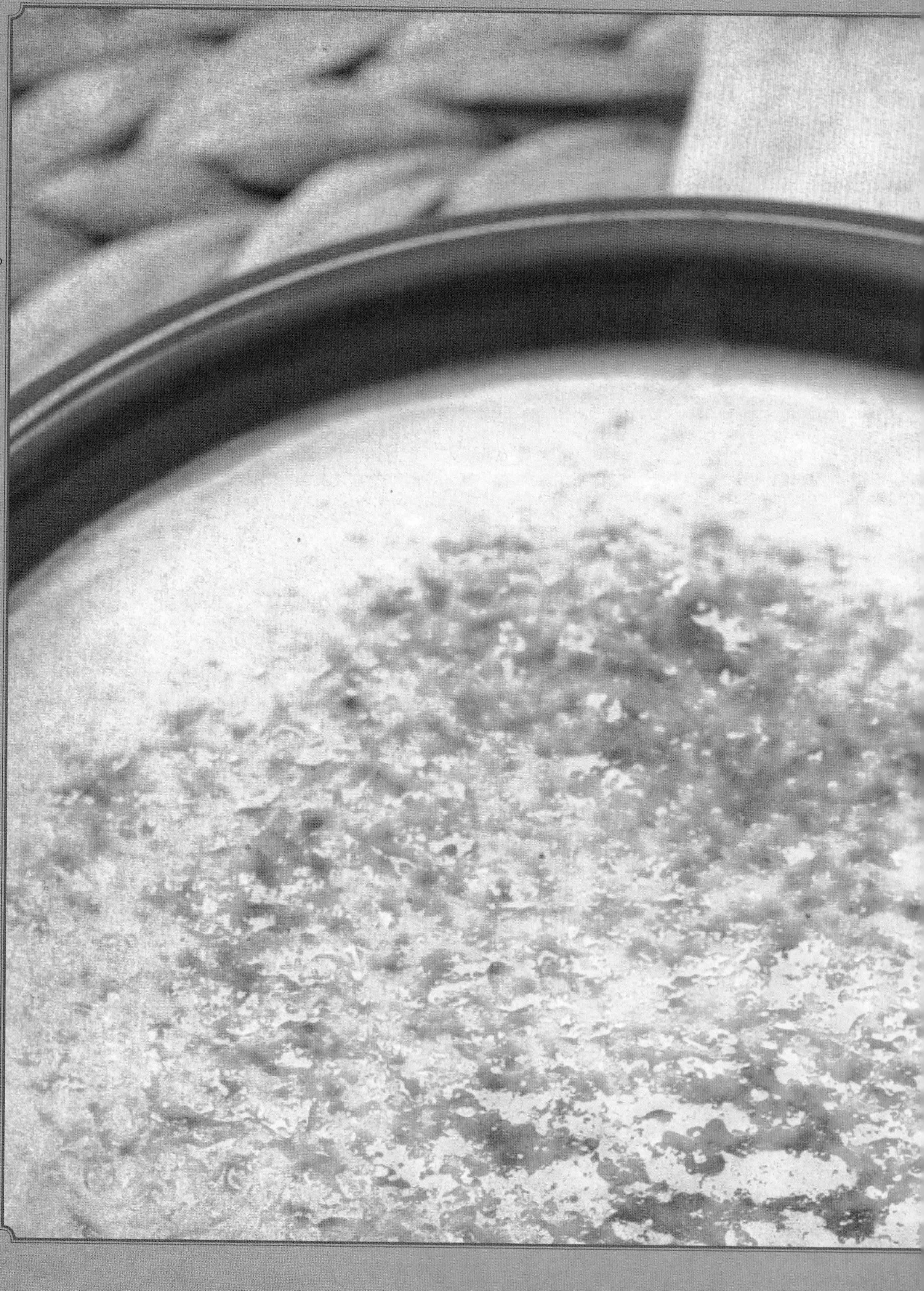

Grain Porridges and Rice Congees

We don't tend to think of "porridges" as a type of soup, but they are actually one of the oldest forms of soup. Whether we use oatmeal to thicken a savory soup, eat it thick with sweetener, or enjoy a congee in the morning to start off the day, we are eating a kind of soup.

I had never heard of congee, which is a type of Asian rice porridge, until I was researching the topic of soups and their origins. While I have eaten my way through many popular Asian soups, I had never tried, let alone heard mention of, congee. I quickly grew to love them. They are often eaten for breakfast and served to the sick, young, old, and everybody in between. While many of us are not used to a savory breakfast (although if you enjoy eggs, that is savory), it makes a very hearty and nutritious way to get your day off to a good start. But really, congee works for any meal.

Plus, I really appreciate how frugal congee is to serve. In fact, many Asian cultures developed congee in part as a method to stretch out limited resources. My limited resources thank congee too.

Every Asian culture has its own version. Some congees are very thin, while others are thick. Some use seafood, some use chicken, and some use eggs. The rice is cooked in a lot of extra liquid until it starts falling apart and is very soft. Then you add a variety of toppings to make it flavorful.

I choose to use white rice for the Thai, Japanese, and Chinese Congee, partly out of respect for the original congees of the world. (You can read about the debate regarding white versus brown rice on page 21.) The Korean Sesame Seed Porridge and the Miso Brown Rice Congee are both made with brown rice, and I've included instructions for making a simple brown rice congee that is easy to use for the Thai, Japanese, and Chinese versions, too.

I predict that we will be seeing a lot more of this popular Asian dish in America in the years to come. It just needs to be discovered.

Chinese Congee
(Zhōu)

4 servings

This version of congee is thinner than the Japanese and Thai versions, and the rice grains are more broken up. Drumsticks are cooked with the rice to create its own broth during the cooking process. Fried garlic, fresh ginger, toasted sesame oil, and soy sauce or tamari flavor it. To make it really special, serve with the Marbled Spiced Tea Eggs (see page 288), which complement the congee well and add more protein to the dish.

1 cup/180 grams long-grain white rice, rinsed

8 cups/1.9 liters filtered water

1 pound/450 grams chicken drumsticks (3–4 drumsticks)

½ teaspoon freshly grated ginger

1 bunch spinach, stem-trimmed, or 4 cups/120 grams baby spinach

2 tablespoons fat of your choice (see page 23)

3–5 medium garlic cloves, peeled and thinly sliced

TOPPING CHOICES

Soy sauce or tamari (use tamari for gluten-free option)

Toasted sesame oil

Grated fresh ginger

Sliced green onions

Ground white pepper

Marbled Spiced Tea Eggs (see page 288)

1. In a large pot, add the rice, water, and drumsticks. Bring the congee to a boil over high heat, turn the heat to low, and cover. Cook for 25–45 minutes (I've left it for over an hour before as well).

2. Remove the drumsticks and any skin that may have fallen off during the cooking process and set them aside to cool.

3. Give the congee a vigorous stir with a wooden spoon to break up all of the soft rice. For a really smooth finish, you could blend it in several batches in a food processor or blender, or use an immersion blender.

4. Add the fresh ginger and spinach in the pot and cook for 3 minutes or until the spinach is soft. Thin with more water or broth, if needed.

5. In a separate medium saucepan, heat the fat of your choice over medium-high heat. Add the sliced garlic cloves and cook, stirring, until the garlic turns yellow. Remove the garlic from the pan with a slotted spoon.

6. Serve the congee with the fried garlic and your choice of other toppings.

GLUTEN-FREE
DAIRY-FREE
Budget-Friendly

Thai Rice Congee
(Chok)

4 servings

This congee is full of contrasting flavors. Allow everyone to add their own toppings. I love mine with a tiny sprinkle of sugar, a generous squeeze of fresh lime, plenty of soy sauce/tamari, green onions, a sprinkle of white pepper, a bit of fresh ginger, and a generous spoonful of shallots and garlic. Flavorful? You better believe it! This dish would still be good without all of the toppings, though.

Regarding the hot pepper, you can get dried Thai peppers online, at Asian markets, and even at some regular grocery stores. They only cost a couple of dollars for a large bag at my local Asian market. However, if you don't have Thai peppers for whatever reason, you can certainly use red pepper flakes instead. The soy sauce or tamari is not optional, as it gives the saltiness factor to the dish.

1 cup/180 grams Jasmine white rice

2 cups/470 ml filtered water

4 cups/.9 liter chicken stock

⅓–½ pound/150–226 grams ground chicken or pork

FOR FRIED SHALLOT AND GARLIC TOPPING

2 tablespoons fat of your choice (see page 23)

6 garlic cloves, peeled and sliced thinly

4 shallots, peeled and sliced thinly

TOPPING CHOICES

4 green onions, thinly sliced

Ground white pepper

4 dried Thai red chili peppers, toasted (see below)

Soy sauce or tamari (use tamari for gluten-free option)

Limes

Sugar (coconut sugar, evaporated cane sugar, or sweetener of choice)

Fresh ginger, peeled and finely grated

1. In a medium pot, add the rice and water and bring it to a boil over high heat for 5 minutes, stirring occasionally.

2. Add the chicken stock to the pot and return it to a boil. Turn the heat to medium or medium-low to keep the mixture at a low simmer. Cook for 20–30 minutes or until the rice starts to disintegrate into the stock at your desired consistency. Stir as needed to prevent sticking and thin the soup with more water or broth if needed.

3. While the rice is cooking, heat a heavy, cast-iron skillet on medium heat. When hot, add 4 Thai chili peppers (if using) and toast them in the pan until they are browned. Remove the peppers from the heat and set aside to cool.

4. For the Fried Shallot and the Garlic

GLUTEN-FREE
DAIRY-FREE
Budget-Friendly

Topping: In the same cast-iron pan, heat fat of your choice over medium heat until hot. Add the 6 cloves of sliced garlic. Sauté, stirring, until the garlic turns yellow. Remove the garlic to a plate or bowl with a slotted spoon.

5. Add the shallots to the pan, sprinkle with a little salt, and sauté, stirring occasionally, until the shallots are soft and browning slightly (about 7 minutes). Remove the shallots to a separate small bowl with a slotted spoon.

6. Carefully crumble the cooled Thai chili peppers.

7. Use a small spoon to drop small spoonfuls of the ground chicken or pork into the rice porridge. Continue to cook until the meat is cooked through (several minutes).

8. Serve with the desired toppings on the side, including the fried garlic, shallots, and crumbled chili peppers.

Japanese Congee with Soy Ginger Salmon (Okayu)

4 servings

244

Japanese congee is typically thicker than other congees. I first learned about it when my parents hosted a Japanese exchange student. She told me how her mother made it and shared an "instant" Japanese congee with me. It had tiny transparent fish in it and was quite fishy tasting. This version is fish based, but not quite as strong. I made my version for her, and she was very enthusiastic about it. That felt like quite a victory to me!

If you prefer, you can beat in an egg or poach it in the congee at the end of the cooking time instead of serving with the salmon. For the salmon, I made one recipe (using ½ pound/226 grams of salmon) and cut the fillet into four pieces for topping the congee. You can also use a little bit of leftover salmon and break it into pieces in the congee to reheat at the end of the cooking time.

Serve this recipe with your choice of toppings. The umeboshi plum paste is a naturally fermented, sour and sweet topping that is quite delicious and good for you. It's worth looking for, and you can generally find it at health food stores. Add just a small amount to each bowl.

Start with about 2 teaspoons of soy sauce in each bowl and add more if desired. Extra ginger can spice things up more, as well as ground white pepper. A spoonful of wild salmon fish eggs adds flavor and nutrition, and green onions brighten it up.

1 cup/210 grams short grain or sushi rice, rinsed well

6 cups/1.4 liters anchovy stock

1 teaspoon fresh ginger, grated

1 bunch spinach or other fresh green

TOPPING CHOICES

Soy Ginger Slow-Roasted Salmon (see page 290)

Sliced green onions

Soy sauce or tamari (use tamari for gluten-free option)

Fresh ginger, grated finely

Wild salmon fish eggs

Ground white pepper

Umeboshi plum paste

1. In a medium pot, heat the rice and 2 cups/470 ml of the stock. Bring it to a boil for 5 minutes.

2. Add the rest of the stock to the pot and turn the heat to low. Cover and simmer for 20–30 minutes or until the rice is quite soft and starts to fall apart. Stir every once in a while to make sure nothing sticks to the bottom of the pan. Thin with more water or broth, if needed.

3. Add the ginger and spinach to the pot and cook until the spinach is wilted.

4. Serve the congee with your choice of toppings.

Miso Brown Rice Congee

4 servings

Miso, a mix of cooked soybeans and rice, is fermented with a particular fungus called koji (or aspergillus oryzae). It's the perfect jump start to soaking or fermenting brown rice to make a more digestible (and tasty) brown rice version of congee. However, you need to make sure you use a miso that still contains live cultures. The label should either say "live cultures" or "raw."

Since brown rice doesn't break down as easily as white rice, I purée this congee in the end to give it a smooth texture. You can use this base for a variety of toppings (like the Fried Shallot and Garlic Topping from the Thai Congee, the Soy Ginger Salmon from the Japanese Congee, or the Marbled Spiced Tea Eggs from the Chinese Congee), or you can just keep it simple with a poached egg, green onions, and ginger.

Umeboshi plum paste is a sweet and sour fermented paste that is delicious and very good for you. It's considered by the Japanese as good for digestion, among many other health benefits. You can find it at many health food stores, occasionally sold in bulk.

As always, offer as many or as few toppings as you like. I would recommend a protein (like the poached eggs), the soy sauce, and the ginger to start with. Add more as desired.

¼ cup/60 ml live-culture miso

1 cup/175 grams brown rice (long or short grain)

1 cup/236 ml warm filtered water

5 cups/1.18 liters chicken or anchovy stock or water

2 teaspoons grated fresh ginger

2 heaping teaspoons wakame (a seaweed available at health food stores and Asian markets) (optional)

TOPPINGS CHOICES

4 poached eggs

Soy sauce or tamari (use tamari for gluten-free option)

Finely grated fresh ginger

Sliced green onions

Umeboshi plum paste

Toasted sesame seed oil

---

1. In a medium bowl, combine the miso, brown rice, and warm water. Mix together and cover. Leave the bowl in a warm place for 12–24 hours.

2. In a medium pot, add the miso and rice mixture along with 1 cup of water. Bring the mixture to a boil for 5 minutes, stirring occasionally.

3. Add 4 cups of stock to the pot and bring it to a boil. Turn the heat to low, cover, and simmer for 1–1½ hours or until the rice is very soft.

4. Add more water or broth, if needed, to thin the soup. I generally add about 1 cup more liquid after the cooking time.

5. Purée in batches in a food processor or

GLUTEN-FREE
DAIRY-FREE
Budget-Friendly

blender, or blend directly in the pot with an immersion blender.

6. Add the ginger and wakame (if using) to the pot and cook for 3 more minutes.

7. To poach the eggs, fill a medium pan with water deep enough to cover the eggs. Bring the water to a boil, drop in the eggs, and simmer for 4 minutes, which is long enough to cook the egg whites, but short enough to leave some of the yolk runny. Remove the poached eggs with a slotted spoon and top each bowl of congee with one egg. Be sure to make the eggs right before serving the congee.

8. Serve with your other chosen toppings.

Simple Brown Rice Congee and Variations

4–5 servings

248

Even though white rice is traditionally used in congees, brown rice does make a very nice congee. In fact, my five-year-old prefers the heartiness of the brown rice versions. The soaking period helps make the brown rice lighter in texture. It will have a mild nutty flavor, and any other ingredient additions will be slightly muted by the brown rice. Because this rice doesn't fall apart as easily as white, I simply purée the brown rice to make a super-smooth congee. This recipe can be adapted to the Thai, Chinese, and Japanese congee recipes.

1 cup/175 grams brown rice (short or long grain)

1 cup/236 ml warm water

1 tablespoon yogurt, kefir, raw apple cider vinegar, kombucha, or other live-culture addition, or brown rice cultured water (see page 296)

2 cups/470 ml filtered water

4 cups/.9 liter stock of your choice, plus extra for thinning the congee

½ teaspoon grated fresh ginger

TOPPINGS CHOICES

Soy sauce or tamari (use tamari for gluten-free option)

Umeboshi paste

Fresh ginger

Poached eggs

Fried Shallot and Garlic Topping (see page 242)

Soy Ginger Salmon (see page 290)

1. In a nonreactive bowl, combine the rice, warm water, and live-culture product. Cover the bowl and leave it for 12–24 hours. At the end of that time, drain the rice and rinse it well.

2. In a medium/large pot, add the rinsed brown rice and 2 cups/470 ml of filtered water. Bring it to a boil for 5 minutes.

3. Add the stock to the pot and bring it to a boil again. Turn the heat to low and simmer the congee for 1 hour.

4. Purée the congee using an immersion blender or in small batches in a food processor or blender. Thin the congee with extra stock to your desired consistency (about 1 cup/236 ml).

5. Add the ginger and cook for 1 minute.

6. Serve the congee with your desired toppings.

For Chinese Version:

Use all water and add 1 pound/450 grams of drumsticks in Step 3. After the cooking time, remove the chicken and cool it before puréeing the soup. Purée the soup and remove the skin from the chicken. Shred the chicken meat and return it to the pot. Save the bones for stock making. Add 1 bunch of stemmed spinach or 4 cups/120 grams of baby spinach and ½ teaspoon of fresh ginger. Cook until the spinach is wilted and serve with your choice of soy sauce or tamari, toasted sesame seed oil, extra grated fresh ginger, fried garlic, ground white pepper, and/or Marbled Spiced Tea Eggs (see page 288).

GLUTEN-FREE
DAIRY-FREE
Budget-Friendly

For Thai Version: After puréeing and thinning the congee to your desired consistency in Step 4, add ⅓ pound/150 grams ground chicken or pork to the pot in small spoonfuls and heat until cooked through. Serve with your choice of toppings, such as sliced green onions, ground white pepper, toasted and crumbled Thai red chili peppers, soy sauce or tamari, lime wedges, sugar, and/or fresh grated ginger.

For Japanese Version: Use anchovy stock and add 1 teaspoon of fresh ginger instead of ½ teaspoon. Add 1 bunch of stemmed spinach or 4 cups/120 grams of baby spinach after you have puréed the congee and thinned it to your desired consistency. Serve it with your choice of Soy Ginger Slow-Roasted Salmon (see page 290), sliced green onions, soy sauce or tamari, grated fresh ginger, wild salmon fish eggs, ground white pepper, and/or umeboshi paste.

Korean Sesame Seed Porridge

4 servings

This nutty porridge can be enjoyed both sweet and savory. It's eaten for breakfast in Korea, just like we eat oatmeal. For a sweet version, top it with a little grass-fed butter and honey. For savory, serve it with soy sauce or tamari (use tamari for gluten-free option) and toasted sesame seed oil. Sesame seeds are a good source of calcium and other nutrients, but don't buy unhulled sesame seeds because they're extremely high in phytic acid. I buy the white, hulled variety in the bulk section of my health food store for about $3 a pound, which makes this porridge fairly inexpensive.

Originally, this cereal was ground with a large mortar and pestle, but a food processor makes it easy. I have tried porridge with both white rice and brown rice, and I prefer it with brown rice for the nutty flavor, which complements the sesame seeds, though it does take longer to cook with brown rice.

1 cup/170 grams long-grain brown rice

1 cup/236 ml warm water

1 tablespoon raw apple cider vinegar, whey, kefir, yogurt, or other live-culture addition

½ cup/60 grams hulled sesame seeds

4 cups/.9 liter water

Dash of salt

White Rice Version

Soak 1 cup/180 grams of long-grain white rice in 1 cup/236 ml of warm water for 20 minutes or up to 2 hours to soften the rice. Process the rice and water together in a food processor until smooth and continue the recipe at Step 3. Cook the porridge for 20 minutes instead of 45 minutes.

Black Sesame Seed Porridge

For a beautiful version of this soup, substitute black sesame seeds for the white.

1. In a medium nonreactive bowl, soak the brown rice in the warm water and live-culture addition. Leave it covered in a warm place for 12–24 hours. After the time has passed, drain the rice and rinse it well.

2. In a food processor, place the rinsed brown rice and 1 cup/236 ml of water and process it until smooth.

3. In a medium saucepan, toast the sesame seeds over medium heat, stirring constantly, until they are lightly browned. Add the seeds to the food processor and process until they become a thick paste.

4. Add the rice and sesame paste plus 4 cups/.9 liter of water and a dash of salt to a large separate pot. Bring the mixture to a boil over high heat. Turn the heat to low and simmer for 45 minutes, stirring occasionally to prevent sticking.

5. Thin the porridge, if needed, with milk or water and add a dash of salt. Stir.

6. Serve with honey, milk of choice, and butter, or soy sauce, tamari, and toasted sesame seed oil.

Irish Yellow Broth

6–8 servings

252

While not as thick as congee, this broth is thicker than most soups because of the oatmeal. I soak my oatmeal with a bit of sprouted flour to add phytase, since rolled oats are generally heat-treated and no longer have that enzyme. I also soak it with a live-culture product of some kind to help it predigest and create an acidic environment for the best breaking down of the antinutrients. (See pages 18–21 for more information about this process.) This recipe does work without the soaking period as well.

1 cup/110 grams thick rolled oats (use gluten-free oats if needed)

1 cup/236 ml filtered warm water

1 tablespoon sprouted flour of choice (optional)

1 tablespoon yogurt, raw apple cider vinegar, kefir, kombucha, or other live-culture product

2 tablespoons fat of your choice (see page 23)

4 carrots, peeled and diced

2 celery sticks, thinly sliced

3 medium garlic cloves, peeled and thinly sliced

1 medium yellow onion, peeled and chopped

8 cups/1.9 liters chicken stock

2 bay leaves

1 teaspoon dried (not ground) thyme or several sprigs of fresh thyme

1 bunch of spinach, well washed and very end of stems trimmed or 4 cups/120 grams baby spinach

Butter to serve (optional)

1. In a nonreactive bowl, combine the rolled oats with the filtered water, sprouted flour (if using), and live-culture product. Cover and leave the bowl in a warm place for 12–24 hours. After the time has passed, drain the oats and rinse them well.

2. In a large pot, heat the fat of your choice over medium to medium-high heat. Add the carrots, celery, garlic, and onion. Sprinkle generously with salt and sauté for 5–7 minutes or until the vegetables are soft, stirring as needed to prevent burning.

3. Add the rinsed oats, stock, bay leaves, and thyme to the pot. Bring the soup to a simmer and turn the heat to low. Add another generous sprinkle of salt and pepper, cover, and cook for 10 minutes.

4. Add the spinach and cook until wilted.

5. Add salt and pepper to taste and serve the broth with a dab of butter in each bowl if desired.

Spiced Moroccan Millet Porridge with Milk

4 servings

Millet is traditionally made into a type of porridge to be eaten at breakfast. You can make it savory or sweet, but for this recipe, I decided on sweet. Why is this in a soup cookbook? Well, grain porridges really are a type of soup! In fact, they were some of the earliest forms of soup. Just because this one is sweet doesn't mean it hasn't the characteristics of a soup. Because I "soak" my millet overnight, it's a bit sour. While the rinsing removes some of the sourness, and the sweeteners and spices balance it out, getting used to a tad of sourness takes time. For that reason, you may want to start with simply soaking the grains without any vinegar or yogurt. By soaking in a warm place with warm water, especially for a longer period of time, you will still get some of the benefits of fermenting/soaking the millet. Of course, the recipe works without any soaking period, too, though I do recommend the soaking. Also, the toasting step both adds flavor and helps to break down the antinutrients.

1 cup/200 grams millet

1 tablespoon raw apple cider vinegar, yogurt, kefir, or other live-cultured addition

1 cup/236 ml filtered warm water

4 cups/.9 liter filtered water

½ teaspoon cinnamon

¼ teaspoon ground ginger

Pinch of ground cloves

Pinch of ground nutmeg

¼ teaspoon unrefined salt

¼ cup/25 grams/60 ml sweetener of your choice (whole cane sugar, coconut sugar, maple syrup, or honey)

2 cups/470 ml whole milk, Homemade Almond Milk (see page 292), or milk of your choice

1 teaspoon pure vanilla extract

1. Combine the millet, live-culture addition, and warm water in a medium nonreactive bowl. Cover and leave the bowl in a warm place for 12–24 hours. After the time has passed, rinse the millet very well with cool water through a fine sieve, drain and set aside.

2. In a medium pot over medium heat, add the rinsed and drained millet. Toast it, stirring, until the water evaporates, the millet starts to make "popping" sounds, and you smell a toasty scent.

3. Add 4 cups/.9 liter of the filtered water, along with the cinnamon, ginger, cloves, nutmeg, salt, and sweetener to the pot. Bring the soup to a boil and turn the heat to low. Cover and simmer the porridge for 25 minutes, stirring every once in a while.

4. Add the milk to the pot and bring the porridge to a low simmer for another 10 minutes. If desired, you can also blend all or some of the millet in batches in a blender or food processor or by using an immersion blender.

5. Add the vanilla extract to the pot.

6. Serve the porridge with extra sweetener, butter, ghee, or coconut oil, and extra milk, as desired.

Chilled Soups

Soups aren't just for cold weather. They can be a refreshing, hydrating dish to serve in the summer, whether a chilled savory soup or a sweet dessert soup.

Many other soups in this book, especially from the creamy vegetable soup section, can also be served chilled. Just make sure that they aren't too thick when serving, as chilled soups are generally best when thin. You can thin a soup with ice-cold water before serving, and salt it to taste, if it is too thick once chilled.

And what is the difference between my fruit soup recipes and smoothies? Not much, in fact. I generally make my smoothies with frozen fruits and blend them into a super thick frenzy. These "soups," however, are made with unfrozen ingredients, and then chilled. Because you eat them with a spoon instead of a fork, you can leave them only partially blended so that you have some texture or you can top them with chopped fruit.

By the way, the Sparkling Mint Melon Soup on page 116 is one of my very favorites.

Tangy Basil Lettuce Soup

4–6 servings

I originally made this soup to serve hot and shared the recipe on my blog. Since then, I've discovered that I especially like it chilled. It makes an elegant, yet frugal soup to serve as a first course. The point of many chilled soups is to whet your appetite. This soup certainly does that. With its refreshing, light flavors, you feel refreshed on a hot day and ready for the main course. You can use a broth or stock, if desired, but I prefer water because it allows the simple flavors to come out without being hidden under layers of stock.

2 tablespoons fat of your choice (see page 23)

1 medium yellow onion, peeled and finely chopped

2 medium garlic cloves, peeled and finely minced by hand or in a garlic press

5 cups/1.18 liters filtered water

2 medium potatoes, peeled and cubed, or ¾ cup/120 grams leftover cooked brown, white rice, or quinoa

1 head of romaine or butter leaf lettuce, washed and cut into thin slices

¼ cup coarsely chopped fresh basil (small handful)

1–2 tablespoons balsamic vinegar

No-Cook Pickled Onions (see page 280) for garnish

Fresh basil for garnish

1. In a medium/large pot, heat the fat of your choice over medium to medium-high heat. Add the onion and garlic, sprinkle them with a little salt, and sauté them until the vegetables are softened (5–7 minutes).

2. Add the water and potatoes (or rice) to the pot and season them with salt and pepper. If you're using potatoes, bring the soup to a boil, turn the heat to low, and simmer it for 15 minutes. If you're using rice, bring the soup to a boil, turn the heat to low, and continue with the next step.

3. Add the lettuce to the pot and cook for 5–7 minutes or until the lettuce is soft.

4. Add the basil to the pot and cook for 1 minute.

5. Add the vinegar to the pot, starting with 1 tablespoon. Add more to taste.

6. Salt and pepper to taste.

7. Blend the soup until very smooth with an immersion blender or in batches in a blender or food processor.

8. Chill the soup overnight or for a few hours until fully chilled. For fast chilling, put the soup in a medium bowl inside a larger bowl filled with ice water. Stir until chilled.

9. Serve with a generous spoonful of pickled onions and lots of fresh basil torn into small pieces.

Chilled Avocado and Cucumber Soup

4–6 servings

260

The cilantro, lime juice, onion, and garlic in this soup make the base flavorful, the avocado makes it creamy and rich, the cucumber adds lightness, and the stock provides even more nutrition. Plus, it is lots of fun to vary the toppings of this soup too! This was a favorite recipe among the recipe testers.

I decided, after some experimenting, that I don't like my soup base spicy, but you can spice it up, if you like, using ¼ to ¾ teaspoon of cayenne pepper. For a slightly crunchy and spicy addition, blend your favorite hot pepper in the soup.

3 small/2 large avocadoes

1 cucumber, peeled and seeded, cut into chucks

¼ cup/40 grams chopped red onion

1 medium garlic clove, peeled and coarsely chopped

Generous handful of cilantro, stemmed (about half a bunch)

Juice of 2 limes

3 cups/710 ml Chicken Stock (see page 44), Light Vegetable Stock (see page 62), Herbed Garlic Broth (see page 66), or combination of stock and water

1½–2 teaspoons salt (less if using store-bought broth)

TOPPING CHOICES

Cooked black beans

Toasted sunflower seeds

Chopped cilantro

Salsa

Tortilla chips

Avocado, cubed and peeled

1. Cut the avocados in half lengthwise. Scoop out the pit with a spoon and scoop out the avocado meat into a food processor or powerful blender.

2. Add the cucumber, onion, garlic, cilantro, and lime juice. Blend until very smooth.

3. Add the broth/water in a steady stream while the food processor/blender runs.

4. Salt to taste, and chill for 1–3 hours (or longer if needed). You can make this recipe 24 hours ahead.

5. Serve the soup with your preferred toppings.

Quick Recipe
Vegetarian-
Friendly
GLUTEN-FREE
DAIRY-FREE
Budget-Friendly

Basil Tomato Chilled Soup

6–8 servings

Tomatoes are used in many chilled soups for a variety of reasons. First, they are available at their ripest when the sun is at its hottest. Second, they are juicy and flavorful without any cooking. The photographed example of this soup is made with both orange and red tomatoes.

This soup takes only a couple of minutes to whip together and requires no cook time, which is perfect on a hot day. I top this puréed soup with a tomato salad, which provides a texture contrast by using the same ingredients in different form. The soup will separate, so give it a brisk stir before serving.

INGREDIENTS FOR SOUP

½ pound/226 grams grape or cherry tomatoes (woody stems taken out; you can leave the little bit of stem on small tomatoes)

1 cucumber, peeled and seeded, cut into 1-inch/2.5-cm pieces

¼ cup/40 grams chopped red onion

1 garlic clove, peeled and roughly chopped

¼ cup/60 ml fresh lemon juice

1 cup/236 ml chicken stock, vegetable broth, or water

½ teaspoon salt

7 large basil leaves

TOMATO SALAD

½ pound/226 ml grape or cherry tomatoes

5 large basil leaves, rolled into a cigar shape and thinly sliced

¼ cup/40 grams finely chopped red onion

1 garlic clove, peeled and finely minced by hand or in a garlic press

TO SERVE

Extra-virgin olive oil

Balsamic vinegar

Ground black pepper

Unrefined salt

1. In a large food processor or powerful blender, purée all of the soup ingredients. You can make it as smooth or as textured as you like. If you process it until very smooth, it will be a little bit foamy.

2. Salt and pepper to taste if needed.

3. If you prefer a colder soup, leave it in the refrigerator for 30 minutes to 3 hours. Alternatively, transfer the soup to a medium bowl and place that bowl into a larger bowl filled with ice water. Stir the soup slowly until chilled.

4. To serve, cut the tomatoes for the tomato salad in half or in quarters and toss them with the rest of the salad ingredients. Sprinkle the salad with a bit of salt.

5. Serve the soup in a pitcher or bowl with the tomato salad, extra-virgin olive oil, balsamic vinegar, and salt and pepper on the side. Let everyone pour, scoop, and drizzle their individual servings, or present each serving premade with each bowl/cup topped with the tomato salad and drizzled with a bit of balsamic vinegar, olive oil, and a sprinkle of salt and pepper.

Quick Recipe
Vegetarian-
Friendly
GLUTEN-FREE
DAIRY-FREE
Budget-Friendly

Chilled Honeydew and Cucumber Soup with Coconut Milk

6 servings

This is a perfect soup to serve in small bowls as a first course. It refreshes you and whets your appetite for the main dish. The soup isn't cloyingly sweet, and the ginger and lime juice add just the right amount of spice without making it too spicy. You can heat it up even more with extra ginger. My husband suggested adding a jalapeño pepper to the mix, which could be quite interesting for those who like it hot.

4 cups cubed honeydew melon

1 seeded and peeled cucumber

1 teaspoon fresh grated ginger

¼ cup/60 ml fresh lime juice

1 cup/226 ml canned full-fat coconut milk

Pinch salt

1. In a blender or food processor, blend all of the ingredients until quite smooth. Refrigerate for 1–3 hours to allow the flavors to meld and the soup to thoroughly chill.

2. Serve in small bowls or cups with small spoons.

Persian Watermelon Soup

4–6 small servings

I love playing with rose water, which is a traditional flavoring agent. It pairs very well with watermelon, creating an elegant pink soup that is a lot of fun. For a different flavor profile, why not try a bit of almond extract and top the soup with a few toasted almond slices? One recipe tester also used 1 teaspoon of vanilla extract with success. The yogurt adds tang, but coconut milk would work well, too.

4 cups watermelon, cubed

½ cup/118 ml whole-milk yogurt or full-fat coconut milk

½ teaspoon rose water

Pinch unrefined salt

Shelled pistachios for garnish

1. In a blender or food processor, blend the watermelon, yogurt or coconut milk, rose water, and salt until quite smooth. If your watermelon isn't very sweet, add a few tablespoons of honey.

2. Refrigerate the soup until very cold (30 minutes to 3 hours depending on how cold your ingredients were at the beginning of preparation).

3. Serve in small dessert bowls or cups with a few pistachios on top.

Quick Recipe
Vegetarian-
Friendly
GLUTEN-FREE
DAIRY-FREE
Budget-Friendly

Quick Recipe
Vegetarian-
Friendly
GLUTEN-FREE
DAIRY-FREE
GAPS-friendly
Budget-Friendly

Zesty Lemon Yogurt and Berry Soup

2 large or 4 small servings

We have beautiful berries here in Oregon, and this soup is a wonderful way to enjoy them when they are at their peak. You could use just one type of berry, but the recipe is especially nice when you use several varieties at a time.

3 cups mixed fresh berries (blueberries, raspberries, strawberries, blackberries, etc.)

4 tablespoons honey, divided

1½ teaspoons lemon zest

1 cup/236 ml plain whole-milk yogurt (I like to use a thin, European-style yogurt; thin with milk if using a thick yogurt)

2 tablespoons fresh lemon juice

1. In a medium bowl, combine the berries with 2 tablespoons of the honey and ½ teaspoon of the lemon zest. If using strawberries, slice them first. Macerate the mixture for 20 minutes.

2. In a separate medium bowl, combine the yogurt with 1 teaspoon of the lemon zest, 2 tablespoons of the honey, and the lemon juice. Whisk to combine well.

3. Smash some of the berries right in their bowl with a blunt kitchen tool like a meat tenderizer mallet or place a portion of the berries in a blender or food processor. Combine the blended or smashed berries with the whole berries.

4. To serve, pour roughly equal amounts of the berry mixture and the yogurt mixture into each bowl from opposite sides at the same time. You can also simply top the yogurt with the berries, and swirl them together slightly.

Coconut yogurt version

Coconut yogurt has a more pronounced flavor. If you use it, I recommend that you add extra lemon juice and/or lemon zest to give the soup more lemon flavor. Otherwise, proceed with the recipe as above.

Spiced Yogurt and Cherry Soup

2 servings

268

A traditional Russian soup using sour cherries, cream, and spices inspired this soup. This version uses the more readily available sweet bing cherries and yogurt, and takes a light hand with the spices. It is one of our favorites. If you can imagine ½ pound/226 grams of cherries blended up with a bit of yogurt, honey, and spices in a bowl, then you can imagine this soup. Serve this in small cups or bowls with a small spoon. Enjoy every bite of concentrated cherry goodness. I have also made this soup with full-fat coconut milk in place of the yogurt, which does give it a more pronounced flavor (but it was delicious too). Thin out as needed.

1 pound/450 grams bing cherries

2 tablespoons honey

1 cup/236 ml whole-milk yogurt, plain (I used a thin European yogurt) or full fat coconut milk

½ teaspoon vanilla extract

¼ teaspoon ground cinnamon

Pinch of salt

¼ teaspoon freshly grated nutmeg or two pinches of pre-ground nutmeg

1. Cut the cherries in half and remove the pits. Toss them with the honey and let them macerate for 10 minutes. Set aside 6 of the cherry halves.

2. In a blender or food processor, blend the cherries with the honey, yogurt, vanilla, cinnamon, salt, and nutmeg until very smooth.

3. Chill the soup for at least 30 minutes or until it's very cold.

4. Thin the soup with whole milk, if necessary, and serve it topped with the reserved cherries.

Mulled Wine and Orange "Soup"

2 large or 4 small servings

This "soup" is more like a thick drink, but whatever it is, you can be sure that it's delicious! It reminds us of a more flavorful version of Orange Julius. Serve it hot in the winter for a drink similar to mulled cider, or serve it chilled in the summer. This is a low-alcohol recipe, as about 60 percent of the alcohol will burn off within 15 minutes of cooking time. Plus, the alcohol is greatly diluted by the oranges. It is one of my husband's favorite recipes.

1 cup/236 ml red wine (sweet or dry)

2 cinnamon sticks

10 whole cloves

2 tablespoons sweetener (whole cane sugar, coconut sugar, honey, or other sweetener of your choice)

4 medium oranges, peeled, chopped, and seeded (about 3 cups)

2 tablespoons Crème Fraîche (see page 282)

2 teaspoons honey

1. In a small pot, heat the red wine with the cinnamon sticks, cloves, and sweetener until the mixture reaches a boil. Turn the heat to low and let it simmer for 10–15 minutes. Carefully strain the wine through a sieve into a heat-safe bowl or measuring cup.

2. In a blender or food processor, blend the oranges and strained red wine until very smooth.

3. Strain the orange/wine mixture into a bowl through a fine sieve. Chill if you're serving a cold soup, or warm the mixture again if you're serving it hot.

4. In a separate bowl, whisk together the honey and crème fraîche, and top each bowl or cup with a spoonful of the crème fraîche.

Quick Recipe
Vegetarian-
Friendly
GLUTEN-FREE
DAIRY-FREE
Budget-Friendly

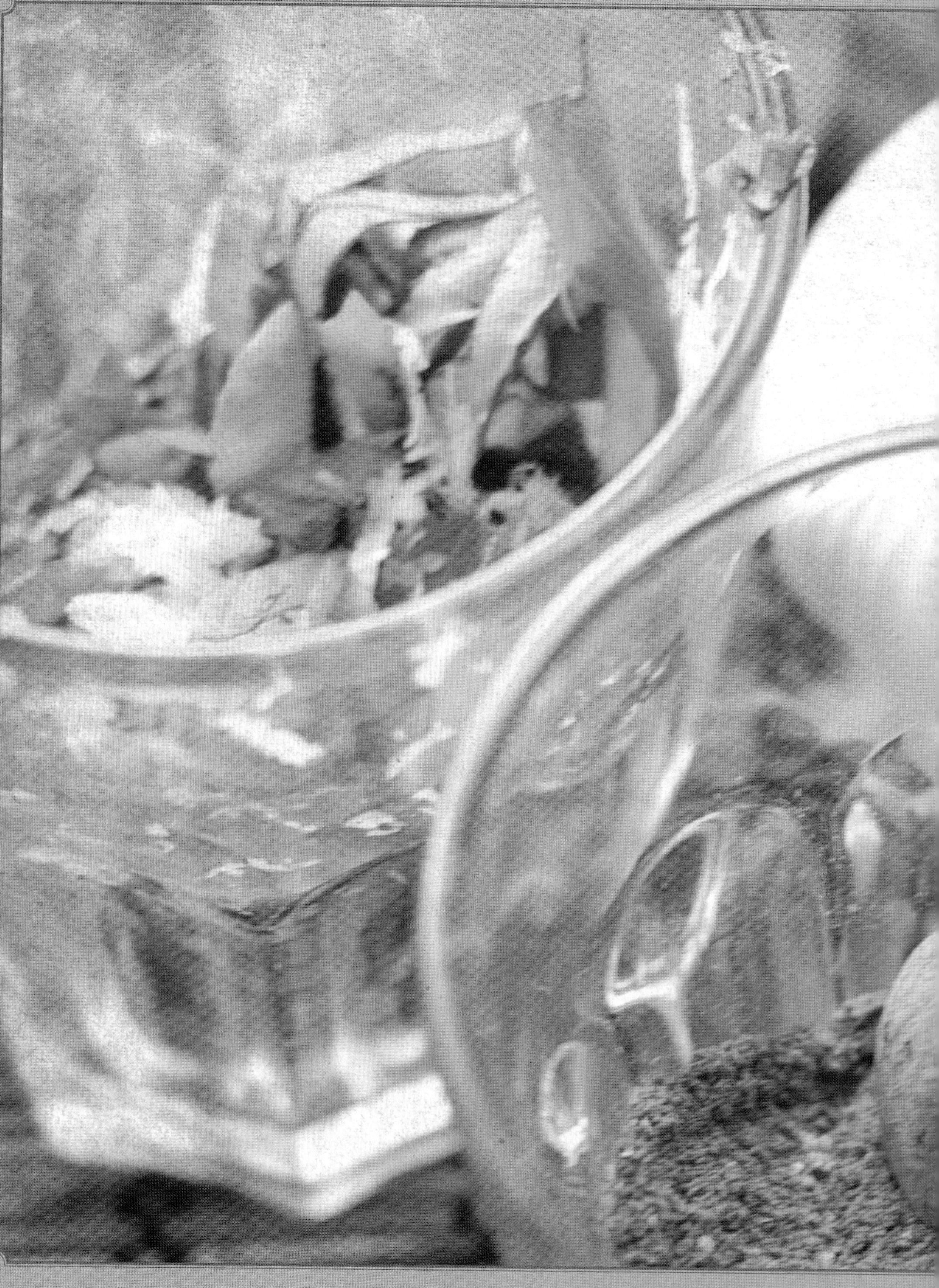

Garnishes, Bacon, Grains, and other Good Foods

This section contains popular garnishes, the meatballs and dumpling recipes used in many soups, and miscellaneous recipes to make your soups even tastier. Certain recipes, such as the Soy Ginger Slow-Roasted Salmon, would also make a wonderful main dish, while others, such as the Marbled Spiced Tea Eggs, make a delicious snack all by themselves.

Delicious Pesto

About ¾ cup

I've always loved pesto, so it's no surprise that so many of my recipes end with a suggestion of dolloping pesto onto them. Pesto is very adaptable. One of my recipe testers mentioned using less cheese, for example, for a more frugal version. Pine nuts are traditional in pesto, but it's surprising how well almonds work. If you have pesto on hand, you can give a variety of different dishes a punch of flavor. The extra pesto will also keep for a long time in the refrigerator in a covered jar. Just add an extra layer of olive oil to it.

1 cup fresh basil leaves, lightly pressed into the cup

¼ cup/30 grams raw pine nuts or peeled and blanched almonds

2–3 small to medium garlic cloves, peeled

2 tablespoons fresh lemon juice

¾ cup/20 grams fresh Parmesan cheese, finely shredded right before using

¼ teaspoon unrefined salt

⅓ cup/80 ml extra-virgin olive oil

1. In a food processor, blend the basil, pine nuts, garlic, lemon juice, cheese, and salt until finely chopped.

2. Add the olive oil, and process the pesto until just blended.

Dairy-Free Version

1 cup fresh basil leaves, lightly pressed into the cup

½ cup/60 ml raw pine nuts or combination of blanched almonds and pine nuts

2–3 small to medium garlic cloves, peeled

2 tablespoons fresh lemon juice

½ teaspoon salt

¼ cup/60 ml extra-virgin olive oil

1. In a food processor, blend the basil, pine nuts, garlic, lemon juice, and salt until finely chopped.

2. Add the olive oil, and process until just blended.

Quick Recipe
Vegetarian-
Friendly
GLUTEN-FREE
DAIRY-FREE

Basil Parsley Gremolata

About ¼ cup

276

Gremolata is a traditional Italian garnish made with fresh herbs, garlic, and lemon zest. It can be used on meats, sprinkled over pasta, or used as a finish to a soup. It's amazing how much flavor it adds!

2 tablespoons minced fresh Italian parsley

2 tablespoons minced fresh sweet basil

1 small to medium garlic clove, peeled and finely minced by hand or in a garlic press

Zest of 1 organic lemon (make sure you don't include any of the bitter white pith)

1. Combine all ingredients together in a small bowl right before serving or garnishing another dish.

All Parsley Version

Use 4 tablespoons of parsley only, no basil.

Garam Masala Spice Mixture

6 ½ tablespoons

Garam masala is a delicious spice mixture. I like to use it by itself to flavor soups, as well as combined with curry powder. Make sure you use fresh spices for the most flavor. You can double it, or make as many recipes as you want of this at a time.

3 tablespoons ground cardamom

1 tablespoon ground cinnamon

1 tablespoon ground cloves

1 tablespoon freshly ground pepper

½ tablespoon freshly ground nutmeg

1. Combine all of the ingredients in a bowl, and store the mixture in an airtight container in a dark place. Use within 6 months.

Homemade Tortilla Chips

72 chips

278

Although you should always be careful when frying anything on the stove, this recipe isn't difficult. You just have to pay attention to the thermometer to make sure you're at the right heat. Frying your own tortilla chips at home is a good idea because you can choose a quality fat to fry them in. Traditionally, beef tallow or lard was used in frying foods. They're stable at high heats and have high smoke points (the point when a fat or oil is overheating and starting to smoke). An expeller-pressed coconut oil is also great for frying. All of these oils have high smoke points and won't break down as much as more delicate fats or oils. Smoke points are approximately: Lard—370F/188C, Tallow—420F/220C, Expeller-pressed coconut oil (not raw or unrefined)—450F/232C. Another expensive new oil option is macadamia nut oil, which has a smoke point of over 410F/210C.

Don't use the hydrogenated lard found at the store, however. Make your own, buy it from a local farmer, or buy it online. You can get instructions on this website as to how to make your own tallow: www.theprairiehomestead.com/2012/02/how-to-render-beef-tallow.html. You can learn to make lard here: www.thenourishinggourmet.com/2009/04/how-to-render-lard.html.

12 corn tortillas (organic and either sprouted or traditionally made with lime)

Pure lard, tallow, or coconut oil

Unrefined salt

1. Cut the corn tortillas into strips or 6 equal wedges.

2. In a heavy-duty pot, add 1-inch of oil. Clip a thermometer on the side of the pot, making sure that the whole tip of the thermometer is submerged in the oil without touching the bottom or side of the pot. Heat the oil over medium-high heat until the temperature reaches 350F–375F/176–190C. (If you're using a cast-iron pan, heat the oil on medium rather than medium-high.)

3. Fry a couple of chips at a time, turning occasionally, until they are crisp and very lightly browned (it takes only about a minute). Adjust the heat, if needed, to keep the oil at the right temperature.

4. Drain the chips on paper towel–lined plates, and sprinkle them with salt.

5. Repeat, adding more fat or oil, if needed, when frying a large amount of tortillas.

No-Cook Pickled Onions

1 cup

I experimented with several ways of making these onions. In the simplest form, I combined 1 cup/236 ml of balsamic vinegar with 1 teaspoon of salt and covered a thinly sliced onion with it. It turned out sweet and delicious! A recipe tester suggested adding water to make it less potent (1 cup of filtered water to ½ cup of vinegar) and adding a little sugar. That variation ended up similar to a Bon Appétit magazine recipe, and I loved it.

When you use raw apple cider vinegar, this recipe also contains healthy bacteria that can help you digest your food. I can imagine adding a lot of different spices to this recipe, both the sweet spices (like whole cloves or a stick of cinnamon) and savory spices such as fennel, anise, or whole garlic cloves.

1 medium sweet or red onion, peeled and thinly sliced

1 cup/236 ml filtered water

½ cup/236 ml raw apple cider vinegar

1½ teaspoons salt

1 tablespoon unrefined cane sugar, coconut sugar, maple sugar, or sweetener of your choice

1. Place the sliced onions in a medium-sized jar.

2. In a medium-sized bowl, mix together the water, apple cider vinegar, salt, and sugar. Pour the liquid over the sliced onions, and cover the jar with a lid. (You may have some extra liquid.)

3. Place the jar in the refrigerator for 1–24 hours before serving. The onions will keep for 2 weeks.

Crème Fraîche

2 cups

This recipe is like a gentle sour cream, rich and creamy with a subtle tang. It's a bit expensive to buy at the store, but it's very easy to culture yourself at home. You need just two ingredients and a jar. It makes an absolutely lovely addition to soup. If you dollop it on top of warm, rather than hot soup, it will keep all of its enzymes, which is an added probiotic bonus. You can use it like sour cream or use it in sweet recipes as well.

2 cups/470 ml heavy cream, not ultra-pasteurized

2 tablespoons buttermilk, live-culture yogurt, or kefir

1. In a sterilized jar (I put mine through the dishwasher), mix the cream with the buttermilk, yogurt, or kefir. Tightly cap the jar, and leave it in a warm place for 1 to 2 days to culture. You will know it's done when it becomes thick.

2. As with all cultured foods, if it smells bad or molds, discard it. (That has never happened to me, however.) It will keep in the refrigerator for 1–2 weeks.

Pan-Fried Croutons

About 3 cups

Homemade croutons are a wonderful, crunchy topping for soups and are so much better than store-bought from both a nutritional and taste perspective. The croutons pictured were made out of a naturally fermented whole-grain sourdough. I love the extra tang that sourdough provides, but this recipes works with gluten-free bread as well.

2–3 slices of hardy bread

4 tablespoons/60 ml fat of your choice (see page 23)

3 large or 6 small garlic cloves, smashed and peeled

Salt and pepper to taste

1. If the crust on the bread is especially hard, cut it off. Then, cube the bread into 1-inch/2.5-cm pieces.

2. In a large saucepan, heat the fat of your choice over medium heat. Add the garlic and sauté it until it has browned.

3. Remove the garlic with a slotted spoon and add the bread cubes to the pan.

4. Gently turn/stir the bread cubes to brown them evenly. When all sides are browned, remove the croutons, and sprinkle them gently with salt and freshly ground pepper.

283

Italian Beef Meatballs

20–32 meatballs

Meatballs are so simple to make at home, and they're especially easy when you cook them directly in a soup! I use pastured (grass-fed) beef to make my meatballs, so they are naturally really lean. I wouldn't recommend using a high-fat-content ground beef unless you were either pan-frying them, or cooking them in the oven, as it would make your soup too oily. (To cook meatballs in the oven, simply place them on a parchment-lined baking sheet, and cook them at 400F/205C for 5–10 minutes, or until cooked through.)

1 pound/450 grams ground beef, preferably grass-fed

2 teaspoons dried Italian herb mix

¾ teaspoon unrefined salt

1 medium garlic clove, finely minced

½ cup/30 grams fresh breadcrumbs (gluten-free bread is fine) or ½ cup/50 grams fine almond flour

1 large egg

1. In a medium-sized bowl, combine all of the ingredients well with your hands.

2. Scoop the meatballs by the tablespoon and gently roll them into small balls. If you use a heaping tablespoon, the recipe will make about 20 meatballs. If you use a scant tablespoon, the recipe will make about 32 small meatballs. Use a melon scoop, if desired.

3. Drop the meatballs into simmering broth and cook them for 5 minutes or until they are cooked all the way through. You can check by cutting one open and making sure it is no longer pink inside.

Chicken Meatballs

20–32 meatballs

I find that Herbs de Provence (Herbs from Provence) is the perfect blend of herbs to use with chicken meatballs. I especially love mixes that contain lavender. So delicious! However, an Italian herb blend will also work well.

1 pound/450 grams ground chicken

1½ teaspoons Herbs de Provence or Italian herb mix

½ teaspoon dried basil or dried thyme

¾ teaspoon unrefined salt

1 medium garlic clove, finely minced

½ cup/30 grams fresh breadcrumbs (gluten-free bread is fine) or ½ cup/50 grams fine almond flour

1 egg

1. Make according to directions for beef meatballs.

GLUTEN-FREE
GAPS-friendly
DAIRY-FREE
Budget-Friendly

Herbed Dumplings

18–24 small dumplings

Dumplings are a simple way to make a soup or stew more filling and satisfying. These dumplings are soft and delicious and speckled with herbs. They can be used in a wide variety of soups and stews beyond my suggested pairings, but, of course, chicken and dumplings are always a favorite. No matter what, I find that my children are much more excited about a soup if they know it will have dumplings in it.

Gluten- and Dairy-Free Version

1 cup/130 grams brown or white rice flour

¼ cup/25 grams buckwheat flour

½ cup/60 grams sorghum flour

¾ cup/177 ml warm filtered water

Scant tablespoon raw apple cider vinegar

½ teaspoon baking soda

¾ teaspoon unrefined salt

1½ teaspoons Italian herbs (or ½ teaspoon each dried basil, dried thyme, and dried oregano) or 1–2 tablespoons fresh herbs such as thyme, parsley, basil, or oregano, finely minced

1. In a large bowl, mix together the flours, water, and vinegar 8–24 hours before you want to make the dumplings. Mix the ingredients until they are well combined, using your hands if needed. Cover the bowl well and leave it in a warm place for the 8–24 hours.

2. When the time has passed, add the baking soda, salt, and herbs to the dumpling mixture and knead with your hands until all ingredients are well combined.

3. Using a tablespoon, drop heaping scoops of the dumpling mixture into your finished soup while it is boiling rapidly (this prevents the dumplings from falling apart).

4. Cover the soup and cook the dumplings for about 8 minutes in a rumbling simmer without disturbing them, or until they are cooked through. Serve right away.

Vegetarian-Friendly
GLUTEN-FREE
DAIRY-FREE
Budget-Friendly

Regular Version

1¾ cups/250 grams whole-wheat pastry flour

1 cup/236 ml buttermilk, thinned live-culture yogurt, or kefir

½ teaspoon baking soda

¾ teaspoon unrefined salt

1½ teaspoons Italian herbs or ½ teaspoon each dried basil, dried thyme, and dried oregano or 1–2 tablespoons fresh herbs such as thyme, parsley, basil, or oregano, finely minced

1. In a large bowl, mix together the flour and buttermilk, yogurt, or kefir 8–24 hours before you want to make the dumplings. Mix the ingredients until they are well combined, using your hands if needed. Cover the bowl well and leave it in a warm place for the 8–24 hours.

2. When the time has passed, add the baking soda, salt, and herbs to the dumpling mixture and knead with your hands until all ingredients are well combined.

3. Using a tablespoon, drop heaping scoops of the dumpling mixture into your finished soup while it is boiling rapidly (this prevents the dumplings from falling apart).

4. Cover the soup, and cook the dumplings for about 8 minutes in a rumbling simmer without disturbing them, or until they are cooked through. Serve right away.

Marbled Spiced Tea Eggs

6 eggs

I love this unusual Chinese way to prepare an everyday food item. The color and flavor of the tea, soy sauce, and spice seep through the cracked eggshells, giving special aromas and tastes to the eggs. They make a lovely appetizer and are also great in soups and congees. While you would suspect that the long cooking time would make these eggs rubbery, somehow they are soft and delicious.

6 large eggs

¼ cup/60 ml soy sauce or tamari (use tamari for gluten-free option)

2 teaspoons black tea (I use pu-er tea, which is not bitter) or two bags of black tea

1 teaspoon Chinese five-spice blend

1. Place the eggs in a medium pot, and cover them with water an inch or two above the surface of the eggs. Bring the water to a gentle simmer for 5 minutes.

2. Remove the eggs gently from the pot with a slotted spoon and run them under cool water. When they are cool enough to handle, use the back of a spoon to crack the eggshells. Aim for a lot of cracks to make an interesting pattern and allow the flavors to seep through, but keep the shells intact. This is the only tricky part of the recipe!

3. Return the eggs to the hot water in the pot and add the rest of the ingredients. Bring the water to a low simmer for 40 minutes. Remove the pot from the heat and cool.

4. After the water and eggs have cooled for about 30 minutes, place the eggs and liquid in a glass jar, and refrigerate. The longer you let the eggs marinate, the more flavorful they will be. Three hours is good, but overnight is better.

5. When ready to serve, gently peel the shells from the eggs, and rinse. The eggs last about 1 week in the refrigerator.

Soy Ginger Slow-Roasted Salmon

2 main dish servings or 4 servings when used on top of congee

This delicious salmon recipe is marinated with Asian ingredients and then slow-roasted. By cooking at a lower temperature for a longer time, you retain the salmon's moisture, giving you flavorful salmon without any of the dryness that many cooking methods tend toward. You can easily double or triple this recipe to make more salmon.

¼ cup/60 ml soy sauce or tamari (use tamari for gluten-free option)

2 teaspoons grated fresh ginger

2 tablespoons coconut sugar, whole cane sugar, or sweetener of your choice

1 large garlic clove, pressed

½ pound/226 grams wild salmon fillet

1. In a small bowl, mix together the soy sauce or tamari, ginger, sugar, and garlic.

2. Place the salmon in a pie pan, marinating container, or plastic bag.

3. Pour the soy sauce mixture over the salmon, and marinate it for 20–60 minutes.

4. Heat the oven to 275F/135C.

5. Drain the salmon, and place it on a baking sheet. Bake the fish for 20–25 minutes or until it has cooked through. To test for doneness, stick a sharp paring knife into the thickest section. If it cuts through easily, the salmon is done.

Everyday Mashed Potatoes

6 servings

Mashed potatoes is one of those dishes that is too often left for the holidays, which is sad because it's a frugal and delicious side dish. It makes a lovely foil for stews. If you'd like to make these especially fancy, try using a naturally smoked sea salt in them. You can just sprinkle it over the mashed potatoes or use it while you mash them. It adds a unique element to an otherwise basic dish.

3 pounds/1.3 kilograms russet, red, or Yukon potatoes, peeled and diced

¼ cup/60 grams butter (for a dairy-free version, substitute a very mild extra-virgin olive oil)

½ cup/120 ml whole milk, cream, half-and-half, or Homemade Almond Milk (see page 292)

1. In a large pot, cover the potatoes with water. Add a generous sprinkle or two of salt, and turn the heat to high. Bring the water to a boil.

2. Turn the heat to low, cover, and simmer for 20 minutes or until the potatoes are tender.

3. Drain the potatoes and return them to the pot.

4. Add the butter and another generous sprinkle of salt to the pot and mash the potatoes with a potato masher.

5. When the potatoes are fairly uniformly mashed, begin to add the milk, starting with ¼ cup/60 ml. The amount you need will vary depending on the type of potatoes you have used and the consistency you prefer.

6. Salt and pepper the potatoes to taste and serve them right away.

291

Quick Recipe
GLUTEN-FREE
DAIRY-FREE

Quick Recipe
Vegetarian-
Friendly
GLUTEN-FREE
DAIRY-FREE
Budget-Friendly

Homemade Almond Milk
4 cups

I have found Homemade Almond Milk to be one of the very best substitutes for cow's milk for many recipes, and especially creamy soups. Store-bought versions are not only full of unsavory ingredients, but many brands taste rancid. This is a rich version that makes a lovely almond milk. If you're using it in a sweet recipe, you can sweeten it to taste, as well as add a bit of vanilla extract. When in a hurry, I've skipped the soaking period with relative success.

2 cups/260 grams whole almonds
2–4 cups/470–950 ml filtered water

1. Place the almonds in a bowl, and cover them with warm water. Add a few dashes of salt (optional; soaking nuts and seeds in salted water is a traditional practice) and soak them at room temperature for about 8 hours.

2. After the time has passed, drain the almonds and rinse them well.

3. Place the almonds with 2 cups/470 ml of water in a blender. Blend for about 1 minute.

4. Strain the mixture using a nut milk bag or cheesecloth over a fine sieve, squeezing well to remove all of the "milk". You can make a second batch of almond milk by taking the remaining almond pulp and blending it again with more water. The second batch will be significantly less rich, however.

5. You will be left with a rich almond "cream." You can thin it with 2 more cups of water for almond milk, or you can use it as is for an especially rich addition to soups.

Basic Quinoa (Soaked)
8 servings

Quinoa is a nutritious, gluten-free pseudo-grain that is delicious and protein-rich. We eat it like rice, topped with butter and sometimes naturally fermented soy sauce. It's also great as a base for stews in place of rice. I find soaked quinoa to be softer on the stomach, and after a long soak overnight, it's easier to rinse off the bitter saponins that coat the grains. Since we eat quinoa a lot, I often soak large batches of it and reheat it as needed.

2 cups/210 grams quinoa

2 cups/470 ml warm filtered water

2 tablespoons yogurt, whey, kefir, kombucha, raw apple cider, or other live-culture addition

2 cups/470 ml warm filtered water

2 cups/470 ml filtered water or stock of your choice

1 teaspoon unrefined salt

1. In a glass or nonreactive bowl, place the quinoa, 2 cups/470 ml of the filtered water, and 2 tablespoons of the live-cultured addition. Cover and leave the bowl in a warm place for 12–24 hours.

2. When you are ready to cook the quinoa, strain it through a fine sieve and rinse it well until the water runs clear. Make sure you thoroughly rinse the quinoa; otherwise, it can be bitter.

3. In a medium-sized pot, add the quinoa, 2 cups/470 ml of the water or stock, and the salt. Bring it to a boil. Turn the heat to low, cover the pot, and cook the quinoa for 15 minutes. Take the pot off of the heat, leave it covered, and let the quinoa cool for 5 minutes before serving.

292

Vegetarian-
Friendly
GLUTEN-FREE
GAPS-friendly
DAIRY-FREE

Vegetarian-
Friendly
GLUTEN-FREE
DAIRY-FREE

Soaked Brown Rice

8 servings

I've always loved the nutty flavor of brown rice. When I started soaking it overnight, I found that it made the rice softer and easier on the stomach. Because brown rice doesn't contain a high amount of natural phytase, it's harder to reduce the phytic acid significantly. You can do two things to improve this: Add sprouted flour to the soaking liquid (try 4 tablespoons in this recipe), since sprouted flour, such as buckwheat or spelt flour, is high in phytase; or make your own phytase-rich soaking liquid by a fermentation process. Instructions are below. (And you can use this soaking liquid in other recipes using brown rice, too!). Replace the cooking water with stock to make a more flavorful and nutritious recipe.

2 cups/240 grams brown rice

2 cups/470 ml filtered warm water

2 tablespoons yogurt, kefir, kombucha, raw apple cider vinegar, or other live-culture addition

2 cups/470 ml filtered water, stock, or broth

1 teaspoon unrefined salt

1. In a nonreactive bowl, place the brown rice, 2 cups of filtered warm water, and live-culture addition. Cover the bowl, and leave it in a warm place for 12–24 hours.

2. After the time has passed, drain and rinse the rice well. Much of the water will have absorbed, which is why you don't need as much water in the next step.

3. In a medium-sized pot, add the rice, 2 cups/470 ml of water or stock, and salt. Bring it to a boil. Turn the heat to low, cover, and cook for 45 minutes without disturbing it.

4. Turn off the heat and let the rice sit for 5 minutes before serving.

Wild-Fermentation Process

This allows natural bacteria to grow a unique-to-rice culture (like a sourdough), which becomes highly effective in reducing antinutrients over time.*

2 cups/240 grams brown rice

2 cups/470 ml warm filtered water

1. Place the brown rice and warm filtered water in a bowl. Cover it with a cloth, and leave it in a warm place for 24 hours.

2. After the time has passed, drain the rice, but reserve ¼ cup/60 ml of the liquid. (Keep it in the refrigerator.)

Vegetarian-
Friendly
GLUTEN-FREE
DAIRY-FREE
Budget-Friendly

3. Cook the rice in two cups/470 ml of water/stock and 1 teaspoon of salt according to the directions above in Step 3. The next time you make rice, add the ¼ cup/60 ml of reserved liquid to the soaking liquid of the rice.

4. Continue the cycle of soaking and reserving some of the soaking liquid. It will become more and more enzyme rich until it can break down an amazing 96 percent of antinutrients in the rice.

Source: http://wholehealthsource.blogspot.com/2009/04/new-way-to-soak-brown-rice.html

White Rice

8 servings

White rice is simple to make and quick, too. Here are some basic instructions. Use these steps for sushi rice, short-grain, long-grain, basmati, and jasmine rice. You can read about the pros and cons of white rice on page 21.

2 cups white rice of your choice
(430 grams sushi rice, 360 grams
long-grain white rice)

2½ cups/590 ml filtered water or
stock

1 teaspoon salt

1. Rinse the rice well through a fine sieve until the water runs clear.

2. In a medium pot, add the water or stock, rinsed rice, and salt. Bring it to a simmer and turn the heat to low. Cover, and cook for 20 minutes.

3. Turn off the heat and let the rice sit for 5 minutes before serving.

Ghee

Depends on amount of butter you start with, roughly ½–1 cup

Ghee is basically clarified butter with all of the milk solids removed. Unlike butter, it can withstand high temperatures and makes an excellent choice when you are sautéing. Secondly, without the milk solids, many people with dairy allergies find that they tolerate ghee better than butter. It's simply a beautiful fat. I make it with grass-fed butter, which results in a vibrant, yellow ghee.

½–1 pound/226–450 grams butter (preferably from grass-fed cows, such as Kerrygold Butter)

1. In a medium pot with a heavy bottom, add the butter and melt it over medium heat until it starts to foam. Turn the heat down to medium low. Watch the butter to make sure it doesn't foam over the side of the pot.

2. As the butter continues to cook, extra liquid will evaporate, and the foam will diminish. When the foam has died down significantly, the milk solids will start to form near the bottom of the pan, and foam will begin to rise again. Watch carefully, as the milk solids will start to brown in the fat. When you see little golden brown bits in the mixture, remove the pot from the heat immediately. You don't want to burn the milk solids. Let the butter cool.

3. Lay a fine sieve over a heat-safe bowl, and lay cheesecloth inside the fine sieve. Carefully pour the warm butter mixture through the cheesecloth. You can squeeze the cheesecloth gently to remove more of the ghee from it once cool enough to touch. The strained liquid is the ghee.

Quick Recipe
Vegetarian-
Friendly
GLUTEN-FREE
DAIRY-FREE
Budget-Friendly

Simple Homemade Bacon

About 2 pounds

If you can rub salt and sugar on a slab of meat, you can make homemade bacon. It really is that easy. Plus, you get the benefits of using high-quality ingredients without any nitrates! Almost all of the bacon that is "nitrate-free" contains celery juice, which is a source of natural nitrates. Ironically, it can be added in such high amounts that these natural bacons have even higher amounts of nitrates. Without any source of nitrates, the bacon won't last quite as long, so I keep mine in the freezer. This recipe is for 2 pounds of pork belly, but you can double the amount if needed. I am able to special-order pork belly from a local store. Local farmers often have it as well, and it is found in Asian markets. Don't eat pork? Try to get your hands on some lamb or goat belly instead.

Experiment with adding different spices to the bacon, such as black pepper, cloves, crushed bay leaves, fennel, garlic, Italian herbs, or whatever else captures your fancy. For a smoked version, try using a naturally smoked sea salt in place of the regular unrefined salt.

2 pounds/910 grams pork belly

2 tablespoons/1 ounce/30 grams unrefined salt of your choice

1 tablespoon/1.2 ounces/15 grams unrefined cane sugar, coconut sugar, maple sugar, or other sugar or your choice

1. Place the pork belly on a large sheet pan.

2. In a small bowl, mix together the salt and sugar, and rub it well all over the pork belly, making sure you cover all sides of the meat.

3. Place the pork belly in a large freezer baggy, and leave it in the refrigerator for 7 days, turning every day or so. Liquid will accumulate.

4. After 7 days, rinse the bacon of the rub, and pat it dry.

5. Preheat the oven to 225F/107 C.

6. Place the bacon on a large sheet pan, and put it in the middle of the oven. Cook for 90 minutes or until the internal temperature

GLUTEN-FREE
DAIRY-FREE
Budget-Friendly

of the bacon is 150F/65C degrees.

7. When done, air dry the bacon in the refrigerator for 12–24 hours on a cooling rack placed over a large sheet pan.

8. Using a sharp serrated knife, slice the bacon thinly or thickly depending on your preference. Any pieces that are unruly can be chopped and used in soups. (Freeze for 20 minutes for easier cutting.)

9. The bacon will keep up to 2 weeks in the refrigerator, or freeze the slices instead. I put together 6–10 slices, wrap them in parchment paper, and put them in a freezer bag in the freezer, where they will keep for up to 3 months.

Resources

I encourage you to buy from local businesses for many of these items. However, I thought it would be helpful to provide a list of websites with a good reputation that sell some of the products in my recipes. There are many places to buy these items online (including Amazon), but I've listed the products' brand website so that you can find out more about them directly from the company. While this list is by no means exhaustive, I hope it's helpful.

Coconut oil

Wildernessfamilynaturals.com

Tropicaltraditions.com

Nutiva.com

Lard, Beef Tallow and Suet, and Duck Fat

Grasslandbeef.com

Flyingpigsfarm.com

Rougie Duck Fat (*available on amazon.com and other online stores*)

Pureindianfoods.com (*ghee*)

Olive oil

Chaffinfamilyorchards.com

Unfilteredoliveoil.com

Delallo.com

Spectrumorganics.com

Seaweed (Wakame and Kombu)

Edenfoods.com

Umeboshi

Edenfoods.com

Goldminenaturalfoods.com

Dried Anchovies/ Sardines

Radiantlifecatalog.com

Amazon.com

Local Asian stores

Soy Sauce and Tamari

Goldminenaturalfoods.com (*Ohsawa Nama Shoya and Tamari*)

San-j.com (*Organic soy sauce and tamari*)

Miso paste

Great-eastern-sun.com (*raw miso*)

Southrivermiso.com/(*raw miso*)

Tomato Products

Bionaturae.com (*strained tomatoes and tomato paste in glass jars. BPA-free*)

Pomi.us.com (*chopped and strained tomatoes, BPA-free*)

Unrefined Sugar

Bigtreefarms.com (*coconut sugar*)

Madhavasweeteners.com (*coconut sugar*)

Navitasnaturals.com (*coconut palm sugar*)

Rapunzel.de (*whole cane sugar*)

Wholesomesweeteners.com (*whole cane sugar—sucanat*)

Unrefined salt

Celticseasalt.com

Realsalt.com

Saltworks.us

Encoreimports.com

Edenfoods.com

Mercola.com

Himalayancrystalsalt.com

Acknowledgments

I am grateful for a wide variety of people who helped support me as I wrote this book. First and foremost, I need to thank my little family. Not only did they have to eat their way through many first attempts of certain recipes and eat hot soup during the summer, but they also had to deal with an often distracted mother and wife as I finished the editing process.

I'm especially thankful for my husband, Joel, who was the one who encouraged me to write this book, comforted me when I was discouraged, supported me when I needed long hours to write, and graciously and uncomplainingly bought cartloads of food so that I could experiment in the kitchen. This book would have never happened without him.

To my two dear daughters, Elena and Aria, thank you for making my life sweet, for giving cuddles, kisses, and hugs, and for helping me keep perspective about the important things of life. Thanks for eating all of my soups, too.

I'd also like to thank the good folks at Victory Belt publishing, and especially Glen, whom I talked to the most. I appreciate the freedom they gave me to develop this book and the kind support they offered as well. I loved having them behind this project.

Thanks to my dear sister-in-law, Sarah, who scrambled over bushes and rocks in search of stinging nettles so that I could make certain recipes. And then, came over and kept me company over steaming pots of soup while we cooked together.

Thanks to my extended family for understanding my busy season of life and for always having an encouraging word to extend. Thank you also for the feedback on titles and different ideas I've had for this book.

Special thanks to my brother-in-law, Shaun Davidson, who took pictures of me and my daughter for this book. He is a far better photographer than I am, and I'm grateful for his help and advice when I've needed it.

Finally, I'd like to thank all of the recipe testers who gave me invaluable feedback. Thank you for all of your patience and hard work. You are greatly appreciated:

Jeanne M. Allgood
Rebecca Anderson
Shelly Atwell
Corinne Ball
Deadra Berkan
Christine Bissler
Melissa Farnham Boyd
Elizabeth Bohn
Crickett Brown
Michele Lewis Cahn
Carter/Mendonca Family
Monika Soria Caruso
Marcia Coakley
Jacqualine Chamberlain

Sally Cordier
Sharon Cupach
Stacy Flatt
Tamara Francis
Pam Grim
Sarah Tullos Hutto
Maryla Trehan
Michelle Jarvis
Krissa Jeldy
Beth Jelks
Valerie Josephson
Christi Lachney
Lia Levy
Amy Love, Real Food Whole Health

Carine Martinez-Goubier
Micaela Marques
Amanda McCoy
Loretta King McElwee
Margaret Mills
Stephanie Morris
Slaney Mullen
Gloria Ocasio
Kathy OHanlon
Planeta Family
Elise Ramsay
Kate Reynolds
Julie Snow
Katie Mae Stanley

Jennifer Stump
Jakki Saul
Leslie Storey
Jill Swanson
Charity Walker
Ida Walker
Samantha Weiss
Diane Wipperfurth
Lisa Youd
Trisha Zimmerman

Endnotes

1 Kimberly Harris, "The Healing Power of Broth," *The Nourishing Gourmet*, September 30, 2011, www.thenourishinggourmet.com/2011/09/the-healing-power-of-broth.html.

2 H. N. Rosen, et al., "Chicken Soup Revisited: Calcium Content of Soup Increases with Duration of Cooking," *Calcified Tissue International* 54, no. 6 (1994): 48688, doi: 10.1007/BF00334329.

3 K. Saketkhoo, A. Januszkiewicz, and M. A. Sackner. "Effects of Drinking Hot Water, Cold Water, and Chicken Soup on Nasal Mucus Velocity and Nasal Airflow Resistance." *Chest Journal* 74, (1978): 408–10

4 Rachel Albert-Matesz and Don Matesz, *The Garden of Eating* (Phoenix, AZ: Planetary Press, 2004), 4.

5 Kimberly Harris, "What's the Fuss about Soaking Grains? Explanation and Research Shared," *The Nourishing Gourmet*, January 16, 2012, www.thenourishinggourmet.com/2012/01/whats-the-fuss-about-soaking-grains-explanation-and-research-shared.html

6 C. Lu, K. Toepel, R. Irish, R. A. Fenske, D. B. Barr, et al., "Organic Diets Significantly Lower Children's Dietary Exposure to Organophosphorus Pesticides." *Environmental Health Perspectives* 114, no. 2 (2006): doi:10.1289/ehp.8418

7 Alice Park, "Study: A Link Between Pesticides and ADHD." *Time*, Monday, May 17, 2010, www.time.com/time/health/article/0,8599,1989564,00.html

8 "EWG's 2012 Shopper's Guide to Pesticides in Produce," ewg.org, last modified June 19, 2012, www.ewg.org/foodnews/summary/

9 Kimberly Harris, "How to Render Lard," *The Nourishing Gourmet*, April 13, 2009, www.thenourishinggourmet.com/2009/04/how-to-render-lard.html

10 Jonah Lehrer, *Proust Was a Neuroscientist* (New York: Houghton Mifflin Company, 2007) 53–74.

Ingredient Index

Kimberly Harris

Kimi Harris is a mother, wife, music teacher, food writer, and recipe developer. She runs the popular website, Thenourishinggourmet.com, where she shares nourishing recipes from the perspective of a busy mother. She is also a featured blogger for Mnn.com, where she writes about food politics and the world of food. In between cuddles with her baby, reading books with her oldest, and the busyness of daily life, she loves to cook healthy food for her family and to share that love with others.